VITAL SIGNS ARE STABLE

M. RUTH SWAFFORD, M.D.

DEDICATION

To My Sweetie, Joe, My Endless Love

CONTENTS

ACKNOWLEDGMENTS

I would like to thank my wonderful husband Joseph for all of his support and encouragement throughout this process. I thank my daughters, Erika Green Swafford and Jessica Marcella as well as my son-in-law, Orrin Marcella, who provided much needed critical comments and assessments. I would like to give a huge thank you to my sisters Verdene Hearn and Alfreeda Spicer who helped fill in the gaps of our childhood and often made me wonder if the right person was putting pen to paper for this story! I would like to thank my Sisters Sipping Tea Book Club members, especially Diane Shakesider who spent countless hours insuring that I was using the King's English appropriately. To my other book club members, Mae Campbell, Connie Carmichael, Toni Fuqua, Marval Hughes, Lillie Jackson, Pretena Knight, Faye Moseley, Rebecca Wills, and Shauna Williams, thank you for your invaluable comments on my earlier drafts. Thank you Ruth Alpert for being one of my readers on my earlier draft. A big thank you goes out to Sue Roman and Sue McGinty for becoming my readers on the final round. Thank you Pauline Field for your inspirational words which gave me the courage to move forward with this work. I would like to give a huge thank you to my copyeditor, Nona C. Strong of Mindful Edits for the innumerable hours that she spent getting this work ready for production.

PREFACE

Isolation is defined as the complete separation from others. Many people think of this as purely a physical state. I surmise that it can be more complex than this, due to lack of access imposed by societal, political, and economic norms. Because we are influenced by all manner of things in our environment, lack of access to any one of them can lead to an isolated existence. Print media was one of the first forms of mass communication. Telegraphs, newspapers, and magazines told of happenings in our country and abroad. Ebony and Jet magazines, first printed in 1945, became the mainstay of news of, for, and about Colored People. Radio, and then television, increased the availability of knowledge about national and international events. Because of the Great Depression and the two World Wars, our country as a whole was living on a shoestring budget. Many obtained food, gas, and other necessities of living by using ration cards. People in our country were already separated by race and religion. Due to the hard times, economics further separated the groups. Women and People of Color occupied the lowest level of existence. Ruth, a Colored girl of the 1940s, was born into this lowest band of society. This is her story.

PROLOGUE

<u>Daddy – May 1979</u>

Squeaky screamed, "Ruth, Daddy's eyes are rolling back in his head."

"Squeaky, get the nurse. Call everyone from home, and go into the waiting room."

When the nurse arrived, I screamed, "Call the code team!"

I had already done my assessment of his vital signs, and there were none. I'd started CPR on Daddy, whose room was located in an annex far away from the central core of the hospital.

I took charge.

Pump, pump, pump, pump, pump, pump, pump, pump, pump -- breathe air into his lungs -- pump, pump, pump -- the cardiac resuscitation mode nicknamed "Dr. Dan," which I had used as a medical student, took over. I was using every ounce of strength and energy that I could muster to start Daddy's heart back.

The code team arrived, laughing and joking. I continued, pump, pump, pump, pump -- breathe --pump, pump, pump -- breathe. Their nonchalance as they entered the room with an ongoing resuscitation in progress was appalling. I could only assume that the expertise of the person doing the CPR didn't matter. After all, it was only a Black patient who was being resuscitated by a Black woman!

The team leader had picked up the chart and was thumbing through it, while everyone else stood around chatting. Silently the nurse tiptoed over to the team leader and whispered in his ear, "The woman doing the CPR is his daughter!"

As he directed someone to take over chest compressions, he blustered, "Ma'am, you can leave. We can take care of this now."

With slow resignation, I trudged out of the room and started down the hall to my family, who were assembled at the end of the hallway, waiting to hear what was going on. They seemed so far away, and each step seemed to take me farther away from them instead of closer. It took only about ten steps before I lost all the adrenaline that had been pulsing through me as I pumped on Daddy's chest. My brother Junior saw me begin to crumble and rushed down the hall. I suddenly realized that Junior reached me just in time to catch me before I hit the floor …

PART I – THE PATH FROM HERE TO… WHERE?

<u>Winter 1950s</u>

Jim Crow laws remain in effect in the South. These laws mandate that whites and blacks drink from different water fountains, use different bathrooms, sit separately in public transportation, and eat separately in restaurants.

When does one begin his or her true dreams of the future? Some may say, "I've dreamed of becoming a movie star since I was a child." Others may have stated aspirations in professional athletics, education, government, or the arts. For African American women who come from simple means, can the seed be planted when they are just pre-school girls? Their journeys are usually fraught with the perils of low socioeconomic status, societal norms, and lack of guidance from role models and mentors. A father with only a third-grade education and a mother with an eighth-grade education during the 1920s could provide only so much guidance toward establishing goals for a different life. Can the improbable journey out of poverty really be actualized?

Ruth's story is peppered with joys, sorrows, injustices, and triumphs. As we take this journey with Ruth, we will be reminded of events that are occurring in the outside world through italicized paragraphs. This information comes from a look back at news snippets found in issues of *Jet* magazine, a primary source of Negro national and society news in the 1950s, as well as previously published historical data. As her journey begins, Ruth has no knowledge of these events.

1 - SMOKEY CITY

I sat on the curb bundled up in my midnight-black mouton coat, whose hood was trimmed in a starkly contrasting white faux-fur to protect me from the blustering, bitterly cold winds of that January morning. As a five-year-old child, my thoughts were not of the future, but of the past.

"Who am I? Where was I before I lived with Momma?"

I knew that I must have been with Momma for a long time because I'd heard stories of how my sisters and brothers reacted when Momma brought me home as a baby.

"Where did you get that little white baby from, Momma?" questioned Gert and Vern.

The color of my skin was in stark contrast to Momma's velvety smooth chocolate-brown skin.

"She hollers too much. Can you take her back, Momma?" asked Boe, the eight-year-old eldest of these three siblings.

Momma had given birth to nine children, and the four oldest had already moved out by the time that I, the baby, was born. Was I really unwanted? Did their words invade my psyche as a baby and imprint upon me that I was unwanted? Were these feelings manifested in other ways as I grew older, resulting in my lack of self-confidence? All of these secret questions pestered me as my journey toward awareness began.

There was no sun in the sky, only dark gray clouds that hung like a death curtain ready to swallow everything up before they released their blanket of snow. I felt prepared, in my warm hooded coat, for the deluge of white that the snow would bring. The snow would light up my world and bring me hours of fun with my friends, the snowflakes, as it covered the mounds of dirt and rocks surrounding me.

"Ruth, come on in and take your medicine before you catch your death of cold!"

Momma was busy preparing all the magical, medicinal potions to ward off the diseases of the winter. Turpentine on a sugared spoon, castor oil floating in a spoonful of strawberry soda, and an asphidity bag to hang around the neck, were just a few of the concoctions she made. My brother Vern lay on the bed in the middle room, after having been up most of the night coughing. I had seen Momma gently smooth the thick goose grease onto his chest in soothing broad strokes. After the goose-grease application, she tore strips of an old muslin sheet to wrap around his chest to prevent the healing grease from escaping. Meanwhile, the pungent malodorous smell of the roots and herbs that went into the asphidity bag had seeped into every crack and crevice of our little shotgun house. This smell had driven me outside to the curb. These rituals of winter had been going on since the trees had seen their leaves shimmying from the tops to the ground before their transformation into thin brown crackling chips. I enjoyed making the crunching sound of the crackling chips of leaves as my foot crushed them further into the ground. The dirt that turned my fingernails black also began its dance of hide and seek. The small sprigs of weeds were almost nonexistent among the mounds of dirt and rocks in front of the house.

"Ruth, I'm not gonna tell you again! Come in now!" The "momma voice" sternly penetrated the two-inch window opening and interrupted my reverie. I knew from that sound that I had better move, and move quickly! With dirty hands stuffed in my coat pockets, I reluctantly left my post on the side of the street to receive the medicinal potion that Momma had prepared.

Our little shotgun house had only three rooms and was aptly named: one could stand at the front door with a shotgun and shoot all the way through to the back porch. The middle room, where Vern lay, contained a black cast-iron coal-burning heater which, when it was at max heat, would turn as red as the ring of fire around the sun during an eclipse. Since this was the primary bedroom for the kids, including grandkids, it contained a double bed, which most of us shared. A rollaway bed was kept in the one-and-only closet in the house. There was a small vinyl couch in this room too, but it was full of slits and holes from years of kids' wear and tear. The couch sat in front of the window, which was rarely opened because it had no

2

screen. According to family lore, Gert fell out of this particular window when she was a baby.

The name of our neighborhood was Smokey City, a "Colored Only" area in Memphis surrounded by miles of "White Only" areas along the Mississippi river. It was a less-than-one-mile rectangular stretch of land, whose main streets were only three in number, whether east to west or north to south. Hastings' east-west boundary was sandwiched between Dunlap and Ayers, but the north-south boundary ran the length -- beginning at Keel, crossing Looney, and ending at Jackson Avenue. Several named alleyways – Castle, Baby Row, Red Row, and more – darted in and out of the main streets. These alleyways were home to multiple double-tenant, single- and double-story multiplex apartment houses.

South of Looney on Hastings Street, there were only two business establishments: the Bier Garten and L. M. Schwab general merchandise store. The Bier Garten was the local bar. Its exterior looked as though a strong wind could tear off the dilapidated boards that served as its walls. A creaky wooden porch on the outside had two mismatched stones as its steps. The gravel area in front was strewn with beer and wine bottles, as well as all manner of other trash. If there were ever a depiction of Sodom and Gomorrah in the modern world, the Bier Garten was the place. Drinking alcohol, smoking cigarettes, whoring, and fighting went on every day, with escalation on the weekend to stabbings and shootings. Death was a constant visitor to the weekend happenings.

Though our section of Hastings Street was no more than four-tenths of a mile in length, it seemed gigantic in my mind. There were at least eight little shotgun double-tenant houses on our side of the street, which was transected by an alley before it ended at Looney. There were even more double-tenant houses on the opposite side of the street because there was no intervening alleyway. All of our tiny shotgun houses faced Hastings Street, and there were no businesses of any sort in our block.

All the families had approximately six to eight children, but all the houses were the same size! This world was my cocoon; I knew nothing of the outside world, the people who populated it, nor any of their happenings. *Jet* and *Ebony* magazines published the events of Colored people's lives, but my family could never afford to buy one. The only newspaper I ever saw was something that had been used to wrap meat from the grocery store.

Mississippi - Winter, 1951 – Men of color are being fined and imprisoned for offenses as small as talking to a white man and asking for a bus schedule. In one such interchange, not only is the person talking being fined and jailed but so is his companion, for being a man of color with him.

Being closed up in the tiny, airless shotgun house during the winter was no fun for my meandering free-spirited mind. Occasionally, I had the company of my equally free-spirited nephew, Orne, who was only two months older than I. We would invent games to play whenever he came over. Once, he convinced me that we could determine who the "Greatest" was by playing the kiss-the-lamp game! In this game we had to take turns seeing who could get the closest to the burning kerosene lamp's hot chimney. We each puckered up and inched closer to the lamp, while making exaggerated smacking sounds. Unfortunately he tipped my stool, and I fell headlong into the lamp! My lips were on fire, with fragments of my precious skin attached to the hot lamp's globe. Of course, the lamp got knocked over and broke, but fortunately the flame went out and did not cause a fire. I wish I could say the same thing about our bottoms! Momma grabbed an old brittle seedling switch and beat us both until red welts appeared on our backsides. To add insult to injury, we both had to use the same tub of water to bathe in before we were sent to bed in the already overcrowded middle room.

Occasionally our play antics would provide supreme embarrassment for my older siblings. One evening, Momma had cooked some pig tails for dinner. Orne and I each took one out of the pot, placed it on a fork, and ran through the house to the front room where my sister had company. We shouted, "Momma, can we have some of these dog tails?" My sister flushed a bright shade of crimson as she tried to explain that our Momma was not cooking dog tails! We then found a space near my sister and her friends, so as to begin a fart contest! That was the last straw! Gert screamed, "Momma, Ruth and Orne are being nasty!" These antics resulted in a seedling switch to our backsides.

Momma was the consummate provider, supervisor, disciplinarian, and comforter. She presented a most imposing figure of a woman. She appeared to stand much taller than her five-foot six-inch height on her beautifully shaped muscular legs. Her hair was swept to one side, with a mix of waves and curls on top created by a combination of hot combs and curlers to smooth out the kinks. Her eyes, though small, had a perfect almond shape and appeared to pierce directly into your very soul, especially if you dared to tell a lie! Having birthed and breast-fed nine children, her breasts were quite pendulous and fell to her belly button, which was always covered by her salmon pink cotton snuggies, a source of embarrassment for the entire family whether they still lived at home or not! On wash days, her snuggies could be seen with their multiple holes hanging on the backyard line to dry. On the few occasions that Momma had to go shopping, she always wore a button-down dress to make it easy for her to get to the "nation bag." A nation bag was a pocketed sash, worn around the waist and next to the skin to safely carry her money. To access the money, she would stand on the outside of a store next to a wall, open three buttons below her navel, push the snuggies down a bit, and open her nation bag. This was the ultimate embarrassment for my brother Robbie, who spent just about every weekend drunk! He would scream, "Momma, stop doing that! People think you are fangling yourself!"

Regardless of snuggies and appearances, my favorite nighttime salve was to slip silently into the bed with Momma and Daddy in order to soothe myself to sleep by rubbing my feet on her soft, perfectly shaped legs and thighs. I could sometimes feel the swat of Momma's hand urging me to move my feet, but the touch of Momma's legs remained the best sleeping tonic ever!

2 - CHILDHOOD SUMMER FUN

I eagerly awaited the arrival of summer prior to my first year of school. There would be no paucity of play companions. Summer adventures and misadventures would be in full swing! As was the case with all the little rent houses on my street, the front room served as both a bedroom for the parents and a living room for company. In winter when it was too cold to sit on our wooden front-porch swing, the front room was our entertainment center. It was the only room large enough to accommodate a small double bed, a divan, a dresser, and a covered stool. The headboard was an intricately carved piece of wood that provided a degree of elegance to the bed. The divan, muddy reddish brown in color, only provided comfortable seating for two. The oval mirror in the center of the dresser had a beveled decorative edge that lit up the room when the sun hit it. The covering of the stool matched the vinyl on the divan. There was one screened, cracked window to the right of the front door; a stick held up this window to allow air to come into the house. The other source of fresh air was from the screen door when the front door was left open. All the screens had multiple tiny holes in them, which matched up with the pockmarked windows that they covered.

The kitchen was the room where Momma could make magic happen with her delicious southern cooking. Its centerpiece was the big, black, iron, potbellied wood-burning stove. The kids were responsible for supplying the wood necessary to build a fire. When the fire inside was at its hottest, the black iron stove turned red, mimicking the color of lava spewing from a volcano. To the left of the back door sat a five-piece dinette set, whose legs foretold of better days, before the rust spots and missing nails from the hinges appeared. The table top was made of heavy red vinyl that was a precursor to Formica. The chairs were covered in a similar vinyl, but years of abuse from the rambunctious antics of eight children and their playmates were evident. Many breaks in the vinyl were held together by gray electric tape in various diagonal slants.

Next to the table was the white icebox, whose small top door guarded the twenty five-pound block of ice. The ice man brought this precious ice by twice a week to keep our food cold. There was also a window on the right side of the kitchen door, with its requisite stick to keep it propped open for air. On the opposite side of the room was a tall, wooden utility table used as a place to hold the dishpan and to chop, cut, and prepare food for cooking. Our little shotgun house, like the rest of the dwellings on the block, was not a place to be inside during a blisteringly hot summer night.

None of these houses had electricity, running water, or toilet facilities inside. Kerosene lamps, with their smoky chimneys, provided light after sunset and, with their flickering yellow lights, dotted the windows of all the houses. We all kept our windows closed tightly in the summer to ward off pesky mosquitoes and in the winter to ward off the cold. For warmth, we used the coal-burning stove in the middle room.

A single-roofed coal storage building was arranged in a unit of three interiors, with the end units each holding coal and the middle unit designated as the toilet area. For privacy, there was a small separate middle door, which led into an equally small room that held a toilet stool perched above a deep hole in the ground. The toilet stool was made such that as soon as one stood up, it would flush the body waste immediately into the deep hole. Nighttime was particularly treacherous because rats would inhabit the cool dark spaces of the coal house toilet. If anyone was brave enough to venture there at night, protocol dictated that a brick be thrown inside prior to entry to make the rats scatter.

In spite of the depth of the hole, the openings in the wall, and the ill-fitting door, the scent of urine and poop were ever-present. These buildings populated the backyards, with each one servicing two to three families.

My brother Boe was the brave one, and he could be heard many times after sunset preaching a sermon while he sat on the toilet!

"Oh Lord, help a brother out! Toilet paper is so rough that I don't want to wipe. My daddy puts me out on the back porch to sleep 'cause I smell so bad. Deliver me, your humble servant, Oh Heavenly Father, from this wretched land," preached Boe.

Momma would eventually go out and say, "If you don't shut up that ruckus, I'll deliver you to your brother's razor strap!"

Boe, whose middle name should have been Trouble, was intimately familiar with the razor-strap punishment. When he was younger, the thought of a whipping made him pee on himself. But that was never enough to keep him out of trouble. One time, I remember hearing him bargaining with Momma to keep her from telling Daddy that he threw a rock and broke a neighbor's window.

"Momma, I've already wet my pants! Now, you don't have to tell Daddy! I'll sweep the yard every day this year if you don't tell Daddy. Please Momma, please?!" It didn't matter how much pleading he did, though; he still got a whipping when Daddy came home.

Whenever he had done some egregious sin, Daddy would pull out the razor strap and beat him. Boe would run under the bed, and Daddy would lift it up with one hand while continuing to whale Boe with the razor strap using the other! Even that could not keep him from running off early in the morning to ride on Mr. Johnny Red's wagon. Boe loved collecting trash with Mr. Johnny Red. Mr. Johnny Red sold his bounty at the scrap yard and generously rewarded Boe with a whole nickel for his help!

Since every wall was paper thin, including those supporting the coal house and toilet, this meant there was very little to no privacy for anyone. For those not brave enough to venture outside during the night to battle the rats, Momma had bought a large, white enamel-covered metal "slop jar," with a top trimmed in red. It sat next to the back door of the middle room for easy access during the night. The task of emptying the slop jar in the morning fell to the older children who were still living at home. As the youngest, I rarely had that duty.

Three feet in front of the toilet stood a gray metal water faucet, whose constant leaks caused muddy indentations in the ground around it. When the muddy holes became too wide and deep, Momma would put wood planks over them for the children to stand on when filling up water buckets for use in the house.

The "decent" end of Hastings Street was always full of kids playing during the days and evenings before bedtime. Picture this typical night. There was one dim light atop a telephone pole. Mothers sat on front-porch swings or brought kitchen chairs out to sit in the yard and go over the daily neighborhood gossip as they watched over their broods. They each used various old metal buckets to build fires, whose smoke made spiral dances upwards as they formed clouds of protection to combat the pesky mosquitos on sweltering summer evenings. Miss Lula, a childless widow, was an integral part of this vigil to watch over the kids and partake of the gossip. Though her coal scuttle was the shabbiest and full of the most holes, her fire provided the brightest light and the tallest billowing plume of smoke in the mosquito wars.

The older kids were having watermelon skating races as they skidded up and down the street on spent watermelon rinds. We younger kids were playing hide and seek in the alleyways between the houses. We also played underneath the houses, which seemed to teeter precariously on tall gray cinder blocks. Everywhere you turned, the night air was full with the sound of crickets and the smell of honeysuckle flowers from Miss Viola's fence on Keel. The games were on.

"You be 'it,' Froggy," someone would announce, and the rest of us would run off searching for the perfect hiding place while he covered his eyes.

Froggy would then shout out, "Ready or not, here I come!"

You could hear muffled giggles everywhere as we laughed at his inability to find us. Invariably, Silky, Froggy's sister, was the first to be found, and she always accused someone – anyone – of telling where she was.

Miss Lula had already set her cot up in the spaces between the houses for sleep, and we dared not topple it over! The alley behind the houses was pitch black, so I confined my search to the front yards and underneath the front of the houses whenever I was "it." I was just too chicken to go into the dark!

The night air was suddenly pierced by the sound of loud screaming and shouting.

"Get out and don't ever come back, you low-down dirty bastard!"

Miss Lena and Mr. Harry were at it again! The sound of crashing glass rang out, and we kids scrambled and were on my front porch in a flash!

"Call the police! Mo' dear's gonna kill Daddy!" screamed one of their older kids who was not playing outside with the rest of us.

My friends Leyan, Silky, and Froggy, who were also their children, started shaking with fear as their eyes took on the size of flying saucers. Momma had them all come into our house, and she cut open the reddest watermelon you could ever lay your eyes on!

Almost in unison, they all said, "Miss Ruth, can I have some?" Yes, Momma's name was also Ruth. She said, "Yes, all y'all can have some."

I then asked, "Momma, can we skate on the rinds when we finish, like the big kids?"

Again, she gave permission. Miss Lena and Mr. Harry's weekly fight became a fading memory as sweet watermelon juice dripped down our faces and seeds fell onto the linoleum under our feet.

Momma said, "Y'all have to clean up your mess before you go out skatin."

Momma was a stickler for cleanliness. She had often made us sweep the dirt in front of our house to make it look neat, even though we had no grass there.

As we filed out, holding our precious white-meat watermelon rinds (the red sweetness had been present all the way down to the rind), we saw Mr. Harry sitting on the step in a drunken stupor, sobbing. Miss Lena had given him a big hickey on the head with the stick that used to hold up the window in their front room.

Momma was usually the first one to put an end to the fun by calling me in to take a bath in that old number-two tin tub. As hot as it was, I could never understand why she made more heat just to warm up some water for me to take a bath. I was going to sweat anyway! That Palmolive soap sure did smell good as Momma scrubbed me down. After I had been dried off, she would rub Vaseline all over me so that my skin wouldn't be so dry. Colored people in that day were particularly self-conscious about the heels of the feet which, without Vaseline, would be lined with gray, ashy cracks lining the skin on our heels! Having been appropriately "greased," I would then put on my cotton panties and a thin white princess slip and go out onto the front porch, where my pallet was waiting for me to go to bed. After all the running and in spite of my reluctance to stop playing, I was asleep as soon as my head hit the thin, lumpy pillow.

On another night of fun, our playtime was not cut short by

Momma but by sirens heard in the distance from the south end of Hastings Street, where the Bier Garten was located. Vern was breathless as he came running through the alley from the back of the house shouting.

"A big fight is goin on at the Bier Garten! Everybody is in the street with knives and guns, cuttin and shootin everything in sight!"

All the mothers began calling out children's names.

"Buckwheat, Froggy, Leyan, Silky, Pretty Thang, y'all come on in this house!"

"Buck, go on home now."

"Ruth, Vern, Gert, come in now!"

The roll call went on until the street was deserted. What a letdown for us kids to have to go and be shut up inside those airless three-room shotgun houses. The outside smoke fires were dying away, leaving only an occasional ember whose red glow did nothing to scare off mosquitoes, which then returned with a vengeance. Momma had placed a thick, long, round wooden stick under the window in the front room to keep it from falling down and to allow some air flow into the house. Several tears in the window screen gave the mosquitoes easy passage into our house. Instead of sleeping on the front porch, I was forced to go inside and lie on the shared bed in the middle room. It was so hot that I had thrown the covers off me and became a veritable picnic for the pesky blood-sucking insects. Momma didn't open the middle room window, since it had no screen. I lay there sweating, swatting mosquitoes, and thinking, "If she opened the window, I could at least get a little air. The mosquitoes are already in here!" Because of the trouble at the Bier Garten, the fun of sleeping outside had been taken away!

Occasionally my oldest brother Robbie would come by when he was "in his cups," grab some covers, and make a pallet on the back porch or on the kitchen floor. Since the four kids at home shared the middle room sleeping quarters, there was no more room inside for another body to sleep.

After everyone had settled in for sleep and hot humid air wafted through the windows, propped open by their wooden sticks, we suddenly heard a loud crash which mimicked the sound of overturned furniture. Then came, rapidly, a voice screaming.

"God dammit Harry, get your drunken ass out of here!"

We knew instantly that Miss Lena and Mr. Harry were at it yet again. The back door on the other side slammed loudly, and then we heard loud frantic knocking at our back door.

"Mr. Robbie, can you come get Mo' dear off Daddy 'fore she kills him?" screamed Leyan and Silky.

My brother Robbie, himself three sheets to the wind, dutifully went over to separate the two, nodding his understanding of both sides of the argument, as Miss Lena and Mr. Harry continued to scream and shout to him their positions on the cause of the fight.

Miss Lena screamed, "This bastard had Pearl up in my bed today while I was at work and then had the nerve to go down to the Bier Garten and brag how he had been all up in Pearl! He had the nerve to come home drunk and lie, sayin that he had been workin today but had lost the money! I'm gonna bust this no good bastard's head wide open with this brick."

Mr. Harry protested, "Man you know how dem niggas lie up there. I ain't said no such a thang!"

Robbie turned to Miss Lena and said, "Yeah, they do lie."

Miss Lena grunted and said, "When I find proof, I'm gonna kill his ass. He don laid up here with me and we don had all these chillun and he do me like that! You just wait, his ass gon be grass, and I gon be de lawn mower!"

Robbie said, "Alright Lena, why don't y'all go to bed now and get some sleep. Let the chickadees get some sleep too. Gimme that brick."

She reluctantly handed him the brick, and Robbie hurriedly exited the war zone and returned to his pallet on our kitchen floor.

Mr. Harry didn't know that we had been peeping through a crack in the floorboard of their house earlier and had seen him banging Miss Pearl while Miss Lena was at work!

Miss Pearl was screaming, "Hit it Harry! Make it sing! OOOOH weeee, use that rod!"

The bed was creaking and cracking so loud that we thought the springs would break at any moment! We didn't have a good view, but we could clearly see when Mr. Harry got up and started pulling his pants up!

Miss Pearl groaned, "Why you quittin so soon? Lena won't be off for two hours. Janie told me that she would go in late so that Lena would have to work later to give you and me some good lovin time! You know she won't rock your socks like I just did! I can't come back 'til next week."

Mr. Harry retorted, "Get on up woman. You know them chillun is outside and I don't want them running in here ketching us."

With wide eyes, Leyan turned to me and said, "pinky-swear that you won't tell anybody."

I didn't really have anybody to tell! She was my best friend, so there was no one else we could have told a secret as big as this! So I did the pinky-swear to make her feel better.

Unfortunately for Mr. Harry, somebody told!

After they quieted down, I heard Robbie come back in the house and knew that we could sleep peacefully for the rest of the night.

Since summers were so oppressively hot, housework needed to be started early in the morning. Washing clothes and linen was no exception. Often, it was a communal affair because neighbors would use it as a time to catch up on neighborhood gossip. Number-three tin tubs, Octagon soap, and washboards were brought out and readied for their tasks in the cleaning process. Water had been boiled on top of stoves and poured into the tubs. Neighborhood women could be seen leaning over their washboards, scrubbing clothes as hard as they could to get the dirt out and then wringing them out.

After everything had been cleaned in sudsy water, tubs were emptied and filled with clean water that contained appropriate "bluing" agent. This agent was supposed to make the white clothes look whiter and the colored clothes look brighter! The final process was to hang everything on the line outside, so that the bright scorching sun could finish the job with the natural bleaching that it provided. This gargantuan chore was usually completed before the kids awakened and were out of bed for the day.

Summer was a particularly fun time for me and all of my neighborhood friends. Leyan was my very best friend making our play time together more special. The spacious play area underneath the double-tenant was where we often played house. Being the free spirit that I was, I constantly climbed the majestic but forbidden chinaberry tree perched above the coal house in search of "play" food. In spite of the promised whipping that I would receive if Momma ever caught me, I climbed it whenever we needed to restore our supplies of make-believe food. Momma, with her "all seeing eyes," caught me many times! Her favorite punishment for me was making me lie on a pallet in the front room. It was worth it because the chinaberry tree provided many hours of fun fake green beans, spaghetti, and meatballs. As I lay on my pallet, I would think of the June bugs and Japanese beetles we had caught and hung from string so that they could fly around in circles to provide "fans" for cooling the "play" house. The lightening bugs that we placed in a jar flew around, providing additional light when the sun began to set. My brain always seemed to be dreaming up some play diversion to make the punishment time on the pallet go by more quickly.

If the days were too hot and muggy to play under the house, Momma would fill one of the number-three washtubs with water for us to use as a "swimming pool." White cotton underpants were the swimming attire of the day. The initial jump into the makeshift swimming pool was quite a shock to our little hot bodies. We all would jump right out, full of goose bumps! This was the start of the runs through the backyards and alleys of Smokey City, which were filled with old cars on cinder blocks, discarded furniture, trash heaps of wood, and various other dirt and dust mounds. Return trips to jump into the "swimming pool" caused the water to become very muddy. Having had no concept of the work put into cleaning the laundry, my friends and I found sticks and branches, and then dipped them into the muddy water. We ran through the yards with our dirty sticks and branches and used them to part the clothes and sheets hanging outside to dry. Mud-spattered sheets were found by their owners at the end of the day. Momma's telephone party-line would be lit up by the evening time, trying to pin the deed on the responsible parties. Unfortunately, if I was named as one of the perpetrators, that would be the end of my fun for the night. Momma would send me on a mission to find three skinny, supple, green limbs which could be braided into a switch. The red whelps appearing on my legs were a reminder to think the next time before muddying up the neighbors' laundry. Punishment after a once-a-week laundry day was never enough to outweigh the joy of the hot summer mischief!

3 - SUNDAY MEALS

Sundays were always especially good days for eating. The sound of Momma beating the steak into fledgling tender morsels with a wooden-handled hammer, and the aromas of fresh percolating coffee and round steak and onions frying on top of the black cast-iron potbellied stove, would dance their way into my subconscious as I tried to hold onto sleep. Momma always chose from a variety of foods for Sunday morning breakfast, including brains and eggs, ham, chicken, grits, steak and onions, rice, and biscuits. My favorite was the round steak that Momma religiously pulverized with her hammer. She used her special flour seasonings mix to coat the steak before frying. Before the steak was completely done, Momma would add onions to begin browning in preparation for the gravy. By the time I jumped out of bed, aromas of the steak and onions simmering in the cast-iron skillet were filling the house. The rice was boiling on the stove and was on its way to becoming the thick gooey rice bed which would adorn my plate with its gravy and sugar topping. The stove also seemed to glow in preparation for the biscuits that Momma was making from flour and lard. After the dough was ready, Momma used a wooden rolling pin to flatten the dough before cutting the individual biscuits with an old tin can, whose top and bottom had long since been discarded. The little pieces of dough left after all the circles had been cut were then melded together to make one big "hoecake," the center of attention in the weekly breakfast battle.

Supposedly, the first one out of bed had the privilege of calling "dibs" on the hoecake. My brother Vern was never the first one up, so usually the honor went to my sister Gert and sometimes to me, or so we thought. A hoecake was not complete unless it had been cut and spread with the homemade butter that my "Big Momma" (that's what we fondly called my grandmother) sent from her farm in Tipton County. Whether it was the closing of the icebox or the clatter of the knife on the table, Vern always seemed to appear just when the hoecake was ready to eat! He always managed to stir up some type of diversion. Before we knew it, he had eaten half of the deliciously buttered hoecake before we could even sit down!

More often than not, I had to be satisfied with some of Momma's biscuits with my steak, rice, and gravy instead of the hoecake. Even though they were smaller, they were still the fluffiest, most delicious bread I could ever eat!

Since Daddy was a preacher and Momma sang in the choir, we always had to be up in time for Sunday school at church. Momma made sure that not only was Sunday breakfast ready before we left for church, but also Sunday lunch and dinner. Therefore when we went to a visiting church, Momma always prepared our snacks and lunch to carry with us. This seemed to be such a waste to me when visiting churches in the country because the "Sisters" of the church would always prepare a huge spread of food for the visiting preacher and his family. However, Momma never allowed us to eat their food! She would make excuses that she had so many children that she didn't think it was right for all of us to eat up the food that had been prepared for the Sunday afternoon social. We would be bustled off to our old car to get the lunch or dinner that Momma had packed for us, while the adults gathered around the table for the Sunday social.

One Sunday, I was determined to get a taste of some of the food that the church Sisters had prepared and sneaked under the red-and-white checkered tablecloth that adorned the table.

When the Sisters had gone to chip ice off the block to fill the glasses, and after checking to see if the coast was clear, I emerged from my hiding place to gaze upon the bountiful spread of food. The table was covered with fried chicken, candied yams, fried corn, okra, fresh green beans, butter beans, collard greens, cornbread, pound cake, and peach cobbler. Just as I was about to grab a chicken drumstick, I saw a big fat gray worm wiggle up out of the center of the collard greens! I bolted for the car, and in my quest to get away, I ran smack dab into the middle of my momma's back as she was turning from side to side looking for me. When I looked up and realized it was Momma, I just knew that I was in for a huge whipping when we got home. When Momma realized it was me who had run into her, she reached down and grabbed me up into her arms! Where was the usual "eye" that promised a great punishment? I didn't know that I had been missing for an hour! She was too happy and relieved to see me to fuss at me.

Realizing very quickly that I had dodged a major bullet, I decided to protect Momma from the worm. I blurted out, "Momma, there was a big fat gray worm in the collard greens! It looked as big as a snake!" The understanding look she gave me and the response of "I know, baby" made me never again question why we couldn't eat the Sisters' Sunday spread.

But the fall would bring all this summer fun to an end.

4 - ELEMENTARY SCHOOL

1952 – The United States Attorney General asks the Supreme Court to outlaw public-school segregation, as proof to the world that the "ideals expressed in the Bill of Rights are living realities, not literary abstraction."

Summer freedom drew to a close, and the older kids lamented the rapidly approaching start of school. I was not among the "lamenters" because now I, too, would be able to make the long walk to school with the group from my neighborhood.

The scorching heat of the sun had caused many of the smaller tree limbs to dry and break off. I used those small enough for me to hold in one hand to draw hopscotch boards in the dirt, instead of the usual practice of running through backyards to disrupt laundry hanging out to dry. I had become a master of numbering the boxes since I knew my numbers better than the rest of my friends. I also learned to count as I stood behind my brother Vern and his friends as they played marbles in their circular boundaries in the dirt. There were usually three of them, who boasted loudly of their prowess and subsequent ability to take all the marbles. They each would count out six marbles and place them inside the circle, in strategic positions. They would then line up outside the circle with "shooters" in hand, to determine the order of play. It didn't seem to matter who went first because Vern had the greatest aim with his "steelies." Most of the time he was able to knock a lot more of his competitors' marbles out of the circle. I can still see the glee on his face as he counted up his increasing bounty of multicolored glass marbles.

Preparing for school to start was and always would be a big deal, even though I only received one new pair of shoes and maybe one new dress to start off each year. Although Daddy worked as a porter in a clothing store, I never had the privilege of buying clothes from there. Momma and my older sister Squeaky sewed well, and hand-me-down clothes would be altered for me. I received one pair of new socks at the beginning of the school year, and a pair of resoled Buster Brown brown-and-white saddle oxfords. For the first year, Momma had also bought me a wide-ruled writing tablet, which helped me to form my alphabets correctly. I also had a long yellow wooden pencil that she had sharpened to a thin point using her butcher knife from the kitchen.

The first day of school arrived, and I couldn't contain my excitement! For the first time in my life, I was going to be attending school like the big kids! I couldn't wait! I ate my cornflakes with sweet milk for breakfast and hurried out the door with my paper sack lunch and tablet to meet up with the group walking from Smokey City to Grant school.

To my six-year-old brain, Grant school was such an impressive, three-story, rusty-brown brick building with its wooden floors. My classroom had small brown wooden chairs whose immovable desks were attached to one side. Under the desktop of the chair was a wooden pocket, designed to hold the tablet and a cup holder for pencils. Each room had a small cloakroom, with hooks on which we hung our coats and umbrellas when the weather turned cold or rainy. Looking at the teacher, with her hair wrapped in a vertical chignon at the back, and listening to her perfect enunciation of words as she wrote on the black chalkboard, was absolutely enchanting. I wanted to be able to look and talk just like that!

Armed with the numbering skills that I had learned with hopscotch and the marbles game, I was ready to tackle the "advanced" lessons of arithmetic. I was like a sponge as I absorbed the information with which my teacher regaled us daily. The addition, and later, subtraction lessons would always be written on the blackboard when we arrived each morning. After putting my things away, I would use the first moments to mentally test my knowledge of the problems on the board so that I could be the first one who raised a hand when the teacher called on someone to answer!

For reading, she would bring out either the "Mac and Muff" series or "Tom and Jerry." There were not enough books available for each of us to have one at our individual places. She would seat us in a circle on the floor so that we could share books as we learned to make words out of the letter sounds we saw. These little books had been used by many a child because the yellowed page-edges were frayed and dog-eared from multiple earlier uses. As the year progressed, our teacher would initiate arithmetic and reading competitions to keep the excitement of learning alive. The prize in one of the arithmetic competitions was a Baby Ruth bar. I was devastated when I lost my namesake bar and vowed that would never happen again! My zest to master all things requiring numbers intensified, and I was counting and adding everything at home. My family didn't appreciate such zeal and frequently screamed at me to shut up!

Arts and crafts helped me learn to tell time. We made a clock by cutting a round circle out of cardboard. We each made numbers out of construction paper, and the best ones were placed on the clock. Two pieces of string were anchored in the center to be used as the hour and minute hands. With the clock's completion, we were slowly instructed in how to tell time. Since I don't remember seeing a clock in our house, this too was a new experience that elementary school brought into my life.

Not only did first grade introduce me to new and exciting information but also to other children who were not from Smokey City. My favorite new friend was a boy named Lafayette, who was my puppy-love object. Whenever the seating arrangement in the classroom was changed, we made sure that our seats were always next to each other. At recess, we would file into the lunchroom. Those lucky enough to pay received a hot lunch for fifteen cents. This was a luxury my family could not afford. After eating, each class went out onto the grassy playground and enjoyed playing dodge ball, ring around the rosey, and catch. We could occasionally catch the beginning of the softball competitions that pitted various classrooms of the older kids against each other. This first year of school was shaping up to be all that I expected and more!

Passing by the "all White" Humes High School to get to Grant Elementary School always resulted in a fight between the Smokey City kids and the Humes kids.

"Hey Niggers, where do y'all think y'all going? We don't allow no Niggers on our sidewalk!" yelled out one of the Humes High boys who felt entitled to the ownership of the walkway.

Invariably a huge rock would find its mark on one of the Humes High boys, and the fight would be on! Though I was only six years old, being in the company of older kids emboldened me. I always felt that I was tough and could kill someone if I hit them too hard.

5 - CHRISTMAS

The Christmas holiday brought our first break from school. My daddy liked Christmas and the idea of buying presents, regardless of the value. This particular Christmas, Daddy came in loaded down with presents, robes for the girls and a set of dishes for Momma. Momma was furious!

She screamed, "I been waiting for you to come home with some money to buy dinner and you come struttin in with this shit! I don't want no damn dishes! I need some more food to feed these chillun!"

Daddy refused to have his joy stolen so easily. He proudly announced that he had used the rest of the money to put down on a Model-T Ford that a man up the street was selling! He was flat broke, and there was nothing that Momma's screaming or ranting could do about it.

Fortunately, my momma's brothers knew that we didn't have much, so they often brought greens, okra, and beans from their farm fields. If one of them killed a hog, he would also bring a ham for our Christmas dinner. This Christmas was no exception! They often decided to treat us kids by giving us a nickel to share, and they always admonished us not to spend it all in one place! They knew that Daddy's preaching jobs were few and far between, and any money earned from those would be meager. His regular job at Bond's clothing store didn't pay very much either.

In addition to raising us kids, Momma also had several jobs, one of which was at Cozy Inn, a small hole-in-the-wall diner that served up all sorts of fried meats, sandwiches, potatoes, sodas, and beer. I am told that while Momma was pregnant with me, my older brothers would take turns taking her to this job on their bicycles at night and picking her up at 1:00 a.m. after she got off. This job did not pay much money, but Momma made up for it by handing food out of the back window to my brothers for them to bring home to the kids.

My oldest brother also ensured that we had toys for Christmas. He worked for Lerner's Home Center, which sponsored the annual Christmas party for underprivileged kids. My brother was a driver for the truckloads of toys sent to the auditorium downtown. Though we qualified, we never went downtown to participate in the actual giveaways because my brother and his friends made Smokey City their first stop. They were the "Santa's" who made sure that their families got the prime picks of the donated toys from Lerner's!

6 - SPRINGTIME

Spring arrived, as did the decrease in threads holding the soles onto the remainder of my shoe. Walking had become a fine art, with the front soles of my shoes flapping up and down with each step. The rubber bands used to hold them together usually lasted only two or three blocks. There were ten long city blocks to Grant School. In spite of this, my first spring as a student at Grant was wonderful, primarily due to the May Day celebration. All the first-grade kids had to dress in all white, but each of the other grades would have a May queen who could dress in any color she chose. Gert had sold the most candy and had become the May queen for the seventh graders. Squeaky had made her a beautiful emerald-green taffeta dress with ruffles around the neck, sleeves, and bottom. My sister never looked more beautiful than on that day! She chose a matching green streamer for all the seventh-grade students to wrap around the May pole. Being a part of the colorful May pole wrapping and dancing transported me to wonderland. We sang, danced, and played in honor of May Day under bright sunshine and azure cloudless skies. Life could not have been better on this day. Unfortunately, a few days after May Day, I learned that kids from our neighborhood had been ratted out! We were in a different zone and could no longer attend Grant. I would have to attend my zoned school, Klondike Elementary, in the fall. And to make matters worse, Lafayette would be moving to Chicago! Another "White Only" elementary school stood in the middle of the route to Klondike, still mandating the daily fights! In my mind, having sharpened our skills on the high school kids, these new elementary school kids would be a pushover. It only took a few beatings by us before they learned their lesson and the heckling stopped.

7 - NEW SCHOOL – KLONDIKE ELEMENTARY

Fall, 1953 – Spurred on by President Dwight Eisenhower, the Secretary of the Navy abruptly reverses the traditional policy of bowing to Dixie segregation by banning Jim Crow at more than 40 Dixie bases.

Nineteen-year-old Henry Aaron is named the Most Valuable Player and breaks the color barrier in Southern baseball.

Transferring to Klondike in the second grade was a new emotional hurdle for me. People told stories about the teachers throwing children against the wall to punish them! Though I felt comfortable fighting older children, I could not imagine defending myself against an adult! My brother Vern refused to transfer to Klondike and went to Carnes instead. My sister Gert did agree to transfer with me for her eighth-grade year. However, it was my sister Squeaky who saved the day for me. She told me that if any of the teachers even thought about throwing me against a wall, she would come over and beat their brains out! Her word was good enough for me, and I was able to get over my fear and march into school each morning as "The Battle Hymn of the Republic" blared over the loud speakers before our recitation of the Pledge of Allegiance.

1954 - In a landmark case, Brown v. the Board of Education in Topeka, Kansas (this name was given to represent five cases before the court that dealt with racial segregation in schools), the Supreme Court declares that racial segregation in schools is unconstitutional.
President Eisenhower adds "under God" to the Pledge of Allegiance.

At Klondike, Momma no longer had to make a sack lunch because I was now on the free school lunch program. Unfortunately for me, I was forced to drink milk with my lunch, which I hated. One teacher had the assigned duty to make sure to enforce the "you must drink your milk rule." I knew that if I took too long, my play time would suffer. After that realization, I made milk-drinking a "big gulp" affair!

Klondike was markedly different from Grant. It was a collection of modern brick buildings with well-lighted hallways and classrooms. Academic offerings also increased in this school environment. We were given reports of our progress every six weeks on a report card, which had to be taken home for our parents' signatures. This proved to be a double-edged sword for my ego! When the other kids and I walked home, we initially shared our report cards with each other. Before long they had no interest in seeing mine because I always had all As! My momma wasn't particularly impressed either and said, "That's what you are supposed to get on a report card!" Even though I rarely did schoolwork at home, none of this dampened my enthusiasm for learning. However, it did decrease my desire to show the evidence of doing it well.

1955 - Rosa Parks, a forty-three-year-old seamstress is arrested for refusing to give up her seat in the Negro section to allow a white man to sit down. The Negro community initiates the Montgomery bus boycott in response to her arrest. The boycott lasts for approximately one year and becomes a pivotal moment in the civil rights movement.

The United States Supreme Court decrees that a plan for desegregation is to proceed with "all deliberate speed," thus starting the process for the end of segregated schools.

Fourteen-year-old Emmett Till is lynched in Mississippi for allegedly whistling at a white woman.

By third grade, I had developed a new crush on a boy named James and subsequently held hands with him through the backs of our chairs. The chairs were light blonde in color and had a levered desk attachment which could be moved up and down easily. Learning, by now, had become very easy for me, and I had to find diversions to fill up my time. With so much free time on my hands, my feistiness resurfaced with a vengeance. I would catch small garter snakes along the way to school and put them in a brown bag to scare the kids in the class room. Flying insects, birds, and other animals were all among my store of scare tactics. Report-card classroom conduct grades took a precipitous decline to unsatisfactory marks!

Things at home began to change. Daddy moved out after my tenth birthday! He went to live with another woman who had her own children. Even though I felt that I was Daddy's special baby girl, I feared his departure would make me lose him forever. I became very insolent, and regular spankings with the strap became standard punishment. Even though it hurt, in my insolence and stubbornness I refused to cry.

Finally one day, after what appeared to be an endless lashing of the belt, my brother Vern said,

"Cry, fool. She'll stop hitting you then."

My stubbornness prevailed, and Momma became too tired to continue!

After a while, Momma decided that we all needed a change, so we moved to the alley behind us, called Castle. At this house, we were happy to have a toilet on the back porch and electricity! No more throwing of rocks to scare rats away from the outhouse! And of course, there were no more smoky gray chimneys to wash.

There was a Holy Roller church approximately three doors down from our new rent-house on Castle. The services at our Baptist church on Looney were nothing compared to the noise that emanated from this little church. One could be walking down the street and hear the sounds of cymbals, drums, horns, and a piano reverberating off the walls. Screaming and shouting could also be heard when any of the sisters began "speaking in tongues"! They wore starched white coverings on their heads and long black dresses that went to the floor. While peeping through the window, I once saw everybody dancing, sweating, and throwing themselves prostrate on the altar! This was unbelievable, since dancing had always been forbidden in our house! Momma made sure that we steered clear of that church.

1957 – Martin Luther King establishes the Southern Christian Leadership Conference (SCLC).

Governor Orville Faubus physically blocks "The Little Rock Nine" from entering Central High School. Federal troops and the National Guard are sent to provide some measure of protection for the students.

My conduct in class continued to worsen and reached an all-time low. I remember quite vividly that my sixth-grade report card had all "As" in my academic subjects each six weeks, but my conduct grades were F,C,C,F,C,C -- all written in red ink for emphasis!

Seventh grade was an equally bad conduct year! I was done with my childhood crush on James and had no interest in anyone else, but Robert Lee was always trying to get my attention. One day, I had taken some flowers in to the teacher wrapped in wet newspaper.

"Well, well, well, look who's trying to be teacher's pet," snickered Robert Lee as I was placing the flowers in a vase.

He then decided to ball up the wet paper up and throw it at me!

"Mind your own business and don't touch me with that paper again," I snarled at him as I threw the wet paper back at him.

Silly boy, he didn't listen and hit me with the wet paper again. I jumped over a chair and began beating any part of him that I could reach with my fist, just as the teacher walked into the classroom. Robert Lee was laughing and trying to protect himself from my blows. Our teacher walked in on the middle of this battle and decided we both should be punished. Robert Lee offered to take my punishment (ahhh young love), but the teacher would not allow it. My palms were beet red from the strikes of the wooden ruler that was used to punish me. As usual, in my stubbornness, I refused to allow a single tear to fall.

8 - SUMMER JOBS FOR TEENS

Tennessee – Summer, 1958 – Thousands of Negro cotton pickers have been supplied and trucked to numerous areas surrounding Memphis. Tennessee, Arkansas, and Mississippi cotton growers will pay them $2.00 per hundred pounds of cotton picked.

As I grew older, summers were not quite so much fun. All my friends were able to go on the buses to pick or chop cotton to make a little money. They were being paid a full three to four dollars per day to chop cotton! Those who picked cotton were paid two-and-a-half cents per pound for the cotton they picked. Even though some of them tried to pad the sack with rocks, the farmers usually recognized the intended deception and would not pay for the full weight. Working from dawn to dusk usually yielded only one or two dollars, which seemed like a fortune back then. Momma never allowed me to go on the working trucks, and I thought Momma had to be the meanest person in the world. However, Momma was a very smart woman and knew how to handle my continuous pouting and begging to go work in the fields. One day she allowed me and some of the neighborhood kids to ride up to the country to my grandmother's farm, where she had a small watermelon patch. Momma allowed all the kids to weed the patch and pick any watermelons that looked ripe. After two hours of this "field work," I passed out and had to be brought up to Big Momma's porch. Momma and the other adults were sitting and talking on the porch when I was brought up from the field and laid down. They were talking in hushed voices, and I could only make out a few of the words as I feigned sleep.

"Buck.......skating. Hospital ....vital.......never woke up."

After we left the farm and were back home, I heard that Buck was dead. It was very confusing because I knew that Buck, Vern's friend, had broken his arm when he fell off his new metal skates that everyone envied. How could a broken arm make someone be dead, I wondered silently. Such heavy thoughts could not tarry in my young brain for long. My time in the watermelon patch did make a definite impression, and my eagerness to join the "cotton picking/chopping" crew diminished considerably.

9 - Y-TEENS

Fall, 1959 – With overcrowding of Brooklyn schools, Negro children are being bussed to surrounding counties.

Anti-integration picketing begins in these areas.

I joined the Y-Teens at the end of my seventh-grade year and won the potato-chip-selling contest during my eighth-grade year. As the winner from my school, I joined other area school winners on a bus trip to Chicago. All I had ever heard about Chicago was that my first-grade friend Lafayette had moved there. It certainly had to be some place very far away -- not as far as the moon, but close! I had never been any place out of Memphis, except to the rural area in Tipton County where my Big Momma lived. I was so excited when Momma and Junior took me to the bus station to meet the other area contest winners bound for Chicago! With all the youthful excitement, I was certain that the walls of the bus station would explode around us! We left during the night, and I promptly fell asleep on the bus.

When I awakened the next morning and realized that we had arrived in Chicago, with its skyscrapers and "L-train," I felt as if I had been transported to a foreign land. There was nothing comparable to either of these sights in Memphis, Tennessee. Our tallest building was probably not more than ten stories tall, and our transportation system was markedly different. It consisted of buses, whose long rods sparked red and yellow snippets of fire as they joined the thin metallic gray electrical wires overhead for power and rolled down the middle of the street on old metal tracks.

All contest winners shared rooms in the YWCA. After the initial thrill of experiencing this new world passed, I was enveloped with an overwhelming sense of loneliness. Grown-up thirteen-year-old girls are not supposed to cry, especially those who had jumped across a wooden desk to fight Robert Lee for throwing wet paper towels at them! As I sat in my room, fighting back tears, a knock came on the door.

"You have a visitor in the lobby" came the voice through the wooden door.

"Who? Me?" bounced through the desolation of loneliness to bring me back to cautious optimism. Who could possibly be visiting me? I hurried out of my room, and as I reached the bottom step, I saw this man across the lobby and screamed "Daddy!" I ran towards him and realized within a few feet of reaching him that he was not my daddy. It was his brother, Ed, who lived in Chicago and had come to check on me at Daddy's request. I had never seen him before, that I could remember, but he certainly bore an uncanny resemblance to Daddy. Knowing that I had some family close eased my loneliness significantly and allowed me to enjoy my weeklong trip to Chicago.

We were treated to multiple sightseeing trips, parties, and shopping excursions for those who had brought adequate spending money. The five dollars that my family had scraped together for me did not allow for very much spending! At the parties, the teenagers seemed to have the coolest dance moves, and I was determined to learn each and every one before I left! The dance hall was located on the top floor of one of the downtown buildings. Its windows gave a view of the assorted tracks upon which the L-train traveled. Even though the noise of the passing trains was loud, it offered no competition for the music to which this crush of young bodies gyrated. We partied as though there were no tomorrow! When we returned home, I was the envy of my classmates as I regaled them with stories of big city life in Chicago. I also made sure my girlfriends knew of the seemingly limitless supply of handsome young boys!

The time was fast approaching to prepare all of the paperwork necessary to enter high school. One of these requirements was to obtain a physical examination by a doctor. I had never actually recalled going to a doctor in my life! This would be my first exposure to a real live professional other than my teachers! His office staff took some of the excitement of meeting a doctor out of me by assuming that my visit was due to an adolescent pregnancy! How insulting! At that point in my life, it was only the "fast girls" who had babies, and they were nowhere near the circle of friends that I had. Even if there had been a fleeting thought of becoming a doctor, those assumptions of the office personnel wiped it completely out of my rebel head! However, I did become more resolute about not becoming one of the "fast girls" who became pregnant teens.

10 - HIGH SCHOOL

1960 – Black students begin sit-ins at the Woolworth lunch counter.

The Student Nonviolent Coordinating Committee (SNCC) is founded. This provides a new avenue for young Blacks to be involved in the civil rights movement.

High school brought different avenues for self-expression, from dancing in school shows to marching as a majorette. I had never taken any music courses, but I had a natural rhythm that Miss Carruthers, the teacher in charge of the shows and majorettes, found worthy of developing. Interpretive jazz dance was my favorite genre, and we used it in most of our performances. As majorettes, we danced to the finger-popping, hip-swinging tunes that our band played. We always put on an energetic hip-swinging, high-stepping, and eye-popping show in our short gold and blue skirt outfits, along with white cowboy boots adorned with tassels.

One of my other major high-school ventures was in appearing Saturday mornings on the prize-winning "Quiz-em-on-the Air" show. Back in those days I had a photographic memory and could recite page, paragraph, and line for an answer to a question. We would read the local newspaper and have weekly radio question-and-answer competitions with other Colored high schools in the city. Our team won most of the competitions, which gave me a sense of pride and accomplishment. After so many years of feeling left out because we didn't have a ranch-style home like my friends who lived in the Klondike area, I now had something I could be proud of.

Home surroundings changed again in ninth grade, with our move to Ayers Street. For the first time, my family had a regulation bathtub on an enclosed back porch, running water inside, and electricity. Momma met and married Mr. Henry, making money not quite as tight as it had been when Momma and Daddy were married. Momma and Daddy had divorced when I was in fifth grade; she now only had one job, working at St. Joseph's Hospital as a salad maker, instead of her usual three jobs.

Daddy still chafed at having to send twenty-five dollars per month child support for my brother Vern and me. In spite of Momma's economic constraints, I never went hungry and never lacked appropriate attire for any of my high school activities.

Though Leyan and I were still friends, I began developing a new crew of school friends with whom to hang around. We were all in advanced placement classes and on the college track; Leyan was not. At school she and I still had some home economic classes together, where we were exposed to the rudimentary elements of sewing and cooking. She was not drawn to any of the extracurricular activities that I was involved in either. Therefore we began spending less and less time together. It was around this time that her brother, Froggy, began dabbling in thievery. He would take the cars that were used in the school auto mechanic shop for joy riding. Then he progressed to shoplifting and stealing from larger stores, which eventually led to several terms in the penitentiary, where he later died. I lost track of Leyan's sister Silky during these years.

My new group of friends who lived in Klondike seemed to have picture-perfect family lives, without divorces, alcoholism, convicts, and money worries. They even took family vacations in their big black cars. One of my new friends, Rachel, related a strange tale to me about one of their trips.

She said it started out as usual with her momma packing food and snacks for them to eat along the way. While lying in the back seat with a blanket over her, she heard her parents talking. Her momma was insisting that they stop so that she could go to the toilet. Her daddy saw a gas station ahead and said that she could use the toilet there while he filled up the gas tank. Just as the car stopped, she heard another voice saying, "I don't need no Nigger money. Get your black ass outta heah 'fore I shoot it off!" She remembered hearing her daddy say, "Yassa suh, didn't mean no harm suh." Her daddy jumped into the car and drove away really fast.

I asked, "What happened to your momma and the toilet?"

"She didn't get to use it," Rachel said.

She had drifted back off to sleep and woke up at their relatives' house in California. The vacation story continued with her recount of their time in California. It was something to be envied -- the ocean, sandy beach, and mountains where her family went hiking. Our car could barely make it to my Big Momma's house without breaking down. I knew that I would never make it to California!

1961 – Freedom Riders (Black and White students) head south to test out laws that prohibit segregation. Angry mobs attack them along the way.

1962 – James Meredith becomes the first Black student to enroll at the University of Mississippi. Ensuing riots compel President Kennedy to send five thousand troops to Mississippi.

As a teenager, I was now allowed to go out alone at night to various school functions. But I knew that Momma would be waiting up for me. Though there was no previously defined curfew, I knew when it was time for me to be heading home. During one of our school outings at a rival school, I met the son of a famous D. J. in town, and he asked for my phone number. Within a few days, he called and wanted to take me out.

I asked if it was okay, and Momma said, "NO!"

I was totally flabbergasted and asked why not.

"Because I said so," was her response.

To which I responded, "But Momma, he is the D. J.'s son!"

She looked at me with her piercing eyes and said, "I don't care if he is Jesus Christ's son, I said you are not going anywhere, and that is the end of it!"

I never found out why she was so adamant about my not going out with him. I suppose she had found comfort in our familiarity with the hoodlums in my old neighborhood and their voiced protection of me from an outsider. Perhaps it had been somewhat reassuring for her to know that no harm would come to me from our own. I had often walked at night, with no sense of fear, to the other end of Hastings while the guys sat on the porch of L. M. Schwab or hung out on the corner. Sometimes I could hear hushed whispers.

"Don't touch that girl, she's Junior Wilson's sister. She's Boe Wilson's sister. She's Vern Wilson's sister." I would strut on by with my nose in the air as if I didn't have a care in the world. I also felt some degree of comfort because I knew how tough my brothers were! I had heard of things that had happened to young kids in other neighborhoods from classmates at school, but never in my neighborhood.

One of the more egregious accounts involved a young girl with "funny looking" eyes. At that time, those type of eyes seemed to have been associated with people who were called "dim-witted" or "retarded." As an adult, I realized that this was a reference to people with Down's syndrome. According to the story, some boys heard screams coming from one of the alleys. The boys ran to investigate and saw another boy standing over the retarded girl, with his pants down around his ankles! Fortunately for her, the boys who heard her screams were a neighborhood gang unto themselves! These gangs ruled the streets of their neighborhood and protected their own, just as my older brothers protected me. And everybody knew it!

Two of the passersby grabbed the bad boy and, having seen an old broom lying in the dirt, began beating him with the broom. We heard that he was beaten so hard that the only portion of the broom left was that which could be held in one hand. When her family found out what had happened, the search began, and he was found hiding under an old abandoned house. He then received another beating from them -- with fists, bottles, limbs, or whatever could be found! I doubt seriously if he ever did that again.

May, 1963 – Planning begins for the March on Washington led by Asa Philip Randolph, who stated that "this would be a voice through which Negro masses protest, and demand."

August 28, 1963 – The March on Washington for Freedom and Jobs occurs, with the support of federal and local government leaders. More than 200,000 Negro and White Americans filled the National Mall, stretching from the feet of Abraham Lincoln to the base of the Washington Monument and beyond. The unifying cry was "Freedom."

☐

Fall -- Senior Year of High School

Fall, 1963 – Governor George Wallace tries unsuccessfully to block Vivian Malone and James Hood from registering for classes at the University of Alabama.

Four young Black girls killed when a bomb explodes at Sixteenth Street Baptist Church in Birmingham which was reportedly used for civil rights organizational meetings.

School started, and we seniors were full of expectations. Football games, parties, and social clubs were our primary focus. I was especially high on life because I had been selected as the drum majorette for our band. My lack of musical expertise did not become an issue until now, when Miss Carruthers announced her selection. The band director almost flipped his lid! His idea of the drum majorette was someone who could lead and direct the band, for which I had absolutely no credentials. Her idea was that it should be someone who could command and put on a show! Fortunately for me, they reached a compromise and had not only a drum majorette, me, but also a drum major, a young man who could lead and direct the band! We were an eye-catching pair in our matching long white pants suits trimmed in gold braid and tall white hats on our heads. He had a long baton to help direct the band, but I had only my dancing talents to lead and direct the majorettes. Alas, we never learned to twirl batons! However, with the "booty-popping," high-stepping, hip-gyrating shows that we put on, nobody missed any batons.

On November 22, 1963, the outside world came crashing into mine.

The school loud speakers erupted with "Quiet, Please! Quiet, Please! An important announcement has just come in. President John F. Kennedy has just been shot! We must all pray for his speedy recovery."

We soon learned that the shooting had been a fatal one and that the charismatic young president had died. I knew very little about him, except that he was the first Catholic President of the United States and was very young, with a beautiful wife. What did the killing of a president mean to us? There was no formal meeting in the school auditorium and no further announcements on the overhead system. Obviously, my school didn't feel there was any need for further discussion. We went on with business as usual.

Winter stretched into spring, and the teachers coordinated small group discussions for college prep students so that they were informed about college preparations and details that needed to be discussed with their families. I knew this was not a discussion that would be held at my house. My nephew Orne had already had his idea of joining the army shot down. None of my sisters or brothers had ever attended college, and some of them had not even finished high school. In addition to that, we had no money for college. The guidance counselor began setting appointments for those who would be going to college. I didn't show up for my first two appointments, and she mentioned that to my "Quiz-em-on-the-Air" coach. I was too embarrassed to tell the counselor that my family didn't have money to send me to college. However, when Mr. Riley asked me directly why I had not been making my assigned meetings, I reluctantly told him that we couldn't afford college. He asked if I would mind if he spoke to my mother about it. I agreed, knowing that this would be an exercise in futility! I was certain that it would be a foreign concept which would be hard for her to accept.

After their meeting, and recognizing the stringent financial conditions in which my family lived, Mr. Riley promised my mother that he would do everything possible to ensure that I went to college. If necessary, he would pay for me to attend college in Memphis, at Lemoyne-Owen. He told her that it would be a shame to waste my intelligence because my family didn't have the money. Several weeks later, I saw a letter from Howard University announcing that I had received a full scholarship to attend college in Washington, D.C. I was absolutely over the moon in my excitement! I didn't know what Mr. Riley had done, but at that juncture, I didn't care! I later found that I had scored off the charts on my standardized exams. So this probably had something to do with bringing me to colleges' attention. After that letter, I received one from Spelman College in Georgia, offering admission and a scholarship. Unfortunately, that did not mean that I could automatically go off to college! Not only did my family have input into this decision, but so did some of my momma's neighborhood friends! Miss Lula was the most vocal, saying: "Ruth, if you let that chile go up yonder, she's gonna come back smokin, drinkin, and a loose woman!"

It took a major family pow wow with all of my older sisters and brothers, along with Momma and Mr. Henry,(My step-father) for the final decision to be made. On the last possible day to respond to the university, the vote was cast. I had permission to go to Howard University in Washington, D.C.!

Orne found a low-paying job as a butcher's apprentice. Leyan became a waitress in a small cafeteria that catered only to Negroes. My college-bound friends primarily went to colleges in and around Tennessee, with the exception of Rachel, who went to Vassar College for Women.

On July 2, 1964 President Lyndon Johnson signs the Civil Rights Act. This landmark legislation prohibited discrimination based on race, color, religion, or national origin.

§ § §

"Success is where preparation and opportunity meet" Author unknown

January 1966 – Interior – Momma's Apartment

My nephew Orne walks slowly up the steps to Momma's apartment, dreading that he has to tell her that he has lost his job. He had been told that one of his white co-workers had accused him of stealing some of the meat that he was cutting as a butcher's apprentice. Orne found him stacking produce cartons, walked over, and promptly punched him in the mouth for lying on him. A huge fight ensued between the two of them. The store manager heard the ruckus and went to break up the fight. The white co-worker was screaming that Orne was stealing and had hit him because he told someone. Without hearing Orne's side, the boss fired him on the spot, but not the white boy who had made the accusation.

This injustice is running through Orne's mind as he knocks on the door to Momma's apartment. Hearing no response, he calls out to her, "Big Momma, are you here?" He knocks again and notices that the door is unlocked. As he enters the room, he sees Momma's arm hanging off the side of the couch with the phone receiver lying on the floor. He starts talking: "Big Momma, I thought …"

He stops, and upon closer inspection, realizes that she is not moving. He notices that blood is coming out of her nose. Her eyes are closed, and she is not responding to him. "Big Momma, wake up!" he shouts. He shakes her a couple of times and then frantically picks her up and starts racing down the stairs with her in his arms, screaming at the top of his lungs, "Help, somebody help!"….

11 - COLLEGE LIFE

My acceptance into college was a first for my nuclear family. Since Howard University was located in the Northeast, Momma and I took our very first airplane ride to Washington, D.C. I can still see her as she stood on the steps of the plane in her navy blue dress trimmed in white piping. I didn't know at the time if she was as scared and excited as I was. We looked out the window and chatted nonstop as the clouds passed below us. We both breathed an audible sigh of relief as the plane touched solid ground in Washington, after appearing to be landing in water as it wound its way downward toward the Potomac River. We took a taxi to the campus of Howard University so that I could check into the women's dormitory. These dormitories were located in a quadrangle formation and were accessed through one main front entrance. When we arrived, all the football players who had arrived early to begin practicing for the upcoming season lounged along the wall in front of the women's dormitories. Catcalls had already started, due to the streams of young ladies checking into the dormitories.

"Look at Momma's baby!"

"Are you a long way from home, little girl?"

"That's an awfully big suitcase you have there! Put me in there so that I can go into the dorm with you!"

The walk from the curb to the front door seemed a mile long. I am sure that my cheeks were a flaming red by the time I had finished walking that gauntlet! We were finally inside, where I was checked into my third-floor room by an upper-class residence counselor. My counselor told me that we were starting at a time when rules and regulations had just been relaxed. No longer did female students have to pass a written test before they could leave campus. In addition, the weekday curfew had been extended to 9:00 p.m. from the previous 7:00 p.m.!

I had been assigned to a room with two other young ladies. My roommates were from Ohio and New York City. My exposure to other people and their hometowns increased at a geometric rate. Everything was so new to everyone that I didn't feel out of place at all. We had shipped most of my belongings in a big, black, steamer-trunk, painted with big white letters with my name and college address. We still had to shop for a few other items for my room. Momma spent two days with me, unpacking, shopping, and getting my room together. On the third day, she called me on the dormitory's hallway telephone to let me know that she was getting ready to return home. We talked for a few minutes, then said our good-byes and hung up. I sat in the phone booth and cried for thirty minutes. I felt so completely alone.

Our first residents-only dormitory meeting was held later that evening. We were informed of the "No males in the dormitory" policy with the exception of Spring and Fall Open House, at which time males were allowed in the first-floor parlor of each dorm. Considering the time constraints and the no-male policy, their rules were more stringent than Momma's!

October, 1964 – Martin Luther King receives the Nobel Peace Prize.

Fortunately, college was a time for new experiences and new friends. Interestingly enough, though I was in a major university, I still did not focus on the life-changing events going on in the rest of the country. I was too busy enjoying my independence, such as it was, and making new friends. Most of the girls on my floor were friendly and outgoing, as were some of the other girls that I met from other dormitories in the quadrangle of buildings.

February, 1965 – In Alabama, 50% of the white population are registered voters. Less than .01% of the Black population are registered voters.

Malcom X is shot to death in New York City.

March, 1965 – Voter registration drives intensify in Marion and Selma Alabama. Twenty-six-year-old Jimmie Lee Jackson is killed in Marion during civil rights marches. Dr. Martin Luther King speaks at his funeral and emphasizes the need to make the American dream of voting rights for all citizens a necessity.

It was during this first year of college that I intellectually realized how poor my family really was! My older brothers would send me a few dollars occasionally so that I could have pocket change. I found a work-study job to supplement my scholarship funds, which didn't cover incidentals. I was also able to send Momma a little extra money from my job because she was still making less than the minimum wage working in the laundry at the hospital. This was supposedly a step up from her previous job as a salad maker.

August, 1965 – The Voting Rights Act is passed, making literacy tests and poll taxes illegal. This lifted some of the many restrictions on voting by Blacks.

Parties and staying up late seemed to be the thing to do. Since I had never had anyone standing over me to ensure that I did school work in the past, I drifted further and further into doing minimal schoolwork. This may have been sufficient for a small-town high school, but I was soon to be rudely awakened to the fact that university work required more diligence. I often overslept and had to throw on a trench coat over my pajamas as I tried to make it to my first class, which was calculus with analytic geometry. Arriving late to that class was a huge mistake! Using the weekends to go to the ever-happening parties was an equally bad decision because I never seemed to have enough time to catch up on the work that I missed. Even though my curfew at the dorm was 9:00 p.m., I still managed to be a member of the "hard-core" party group who partied late and found inventive ways to sneak back into the dormitory after curfew. These poor decisions eventually resulted in my loss of the full scholarship that I had received, and I knew that I had to formulate a plan for positive change. My ability to excel without effort had been left behind in Memphis! My momma and family would be so disappointed when they found out how I had allowed my grades to sink into the toilet. Miss Lula's words resonated in my brain: "Ruth, if you let that chile go up yonder, she's gonna come back smokin, drinkin, and a loose woman!" I did not want to go home in disgrace. It was in this sentinel moment that I took stock of my life. I saw where I'd started and where I was now, and decided that I needed to bear down and make more effort to succeed.

This was a rare but beautifully cold crisp day in January for Washington, D.C. The sun shone so brightly that it likened itself to its very beginnings when the Earth was created, without the effect of smog and pollutants. I lay in the dorm room, basking in the moment and visualizing the warmth of being home in two weeks for semester break. My reverie was broken by the shout from down the hall.

"Ruth, telephone!"

Each dormitory floor had only one telephone booth, located at the end of the hall, for all of its forty inhabitants. We spent an inordinate amount of time devising ways to get around paying for our long-distance calls on these phones. One of the most inventive was the design of the long piece of cardboard that we would place inside the quarter slot so that when pennies were put in, the machine registered them as quarters! We couldn't believe that the telephone company allowed them to stay in after receiving so many pennies when they were emptied. We all rode that bus as long as we could.

After hearing my name,   I jumped out of bed, ran down the hall, and picked up the phone.

"Hello," I gasped into the phone while trying to catch my breath.

"Hello, I was just thinking about you and wanted to hear your voice," I heard Momma say.

Guiltily, I began promising that my grades would be better the next semester than they were right now. Momma listened quietly. I also began relating stories of my new-found friends. Sarita -- with huge gray eyes, from North Carolina -- was very considerate and friendly to everyone. She had a smile and a willingness to help anyone who needed it. Norma, who had a quiet elegance about herself, was a classical pianist from Oklahoma. I couldn't identify with the music she played, but it had a calming quality about it. Ronaldo, a brash, self-assured young man from Florida, always had a game to run. I would join him and some of his other friends in the cafeteria to play Tonk (a card game) for money. He never figured out that I grew up on Tonk at home, watching my older sisters and brothers play, from the time that I was tall enough to peep over the card table! Belinda, a short little fireball, and Mabel, a shy quiet young lady, were from Texas. This group was similar to my high school friends, but markedly different from Leyan, who had found a job working in a cafeteria after high school because she did not want to go to college.

"I'm glad to hear that you are not alone," Momma said.

"No, I'm not, but I am really happy that our break is coming up soon. I really miss your fried chicken and collard greens."

"We'll have some ready when you come home. Now, you be good and be careful up there. Please watch your mouth! I don't want you locked up because your mouth got you in trouble!"

With that, the conversation ended. I ran over to Belinda's room where Mabel and Norma were talking and told them that I had just finished talking to my momma.

"In the middle of the day?" one of them said.

"Yes it was a little strange, and I had the impression that Momma really wanted me to come home. Maybe I should go home now. Do you guys have any extra cash?"

After checking all purses and pockets, they could only come up with ten dollars, not even enough for a bus ticket! Oh, well, semester break was only two weeks away ...

Mr. Dee's sundry was the campus hangout down on Irving Street. I was sitting in one of the three cramped orange, vinyl-covered booths shooting the breeze when Ronaldo ran in to tell me that I was needed back at the dorm right away. Thinking that he just wanted my seat and was running a game, I asked why. He said, "I don't know, but everybody has been looking for you!" The look in his eyes told me that he was serious. With that, I got up and sprinted the several blocks to the dorm, arrived out of breath, and found Sarita and my dorm counselor packing my suitcase.

"What's going on?" I asked.

Sarita said "Your brother Junior called the office and told Mrs. Withers, the dorm counselor, that you needed to come home right away."

The suitcase had just been closed when Rev. and Mrs. Thurston, my boyfriend's parents, drove up to take me to the airport. The weather had shifted to bitterly cold, with snowy and treacherously icy roads. This made travel very slow, and their absence of conversation made it seem like a very long car ride. The weather change had also resulted in flight delays. As I waited, I decided to call Sarita and tell her that I had arrived home.

Sarita said in a very subdued and questioning voice, "Really"?

"Of course" I quipped cheerily. "These newfangled things called airplanes can get you there in a few minutes!"

There was an awkward silence broken by Sarita's question, "How is your mom?"

"My mom?" I said.

"Yes," Sarita replied.

Another pregnant silence occurred before Sarita found her voice again to ask,

"You are not really home, are you?"

I said," Why are you asking me these things"?

Sarita replied, "I'm sorry sweetie, but your brother told us not to say anything. Your mom is in the hospital."

My chest tried to close up on me and stop my breathing. The phone booth that I was in became stifling. I hurriedly ended the conversation and went to my gate to await clearance for boarding and departure. Thus began my silent pleading with God to watch over my momma until I could get there.

The airplane ride was interminably long and filled with my continuing prayers and silent tears.

Upon arrival, Vern, Gert, and Jobie met me at the gate. As we went down the escalator, Vern said, "It doesn't look good for Momma."

Gigantic waterfalls of tears began cascading down my face and cut off my voice. We all climbed into the car to head for the hospital, and drove down the dirty, snow-covered streets which hid treacherous patches of ice. Upon arriving at the hospital we went into Momma's room. Momma was lying there covered with a white sheet, her eyes closed, and a tube coming out of her mouth. She was connected to a Bird ventilator, which made little whistling sounds as it forced air into her lungs. Squeaky, with red puffy eyes and silent tears, sat at the bedside rocking back and forth as she gently caressed Momma's legs. I went to the other side of the bed and touched Momma's right leg, which was warm to the touch. That touch gave me the familiar comfort I used to feel when I would sneak into Momma's bed at night and rub my feet against her leg.

"What happened?" I asked.

I was told that my nephew Orne had gone upstairs to our apartment earlier that day and found Momma lying still on the couch, with the telephone receiver on the floor and blood coming from her nose. He had picked her up and run downstairs with her in his arms screaming for help. A neighbor had put them in his car and driven them to the emergency room. In that moment, I realized that I had been the last person to talk to Momma. My chest began to rebel again. There was not enough air in the room. My big brother Junior led me gently into the hallway. Amid my protests, he insisted that I go home and get some rest.

After a restless night, Orne awakened me early the next morning and told me that Junior wanted everyone at the hospital.

Dr. Haynes was at the foot of Momma's bed when we arrived. As we all took up our posts around Momma's bed, each touching some part of her body as she lay there, the doctor spoke to us and said, "There is nothing else that can be done for her. Certainly, she feels warm to your touch and her vital signs look stable because her heart is still pumping and the ventilator is breathing for her. But she will never be able to wake up."

I interjected, "But she's so warm, and I can feel her heart beating. She's just sleeping."

He repeated, "I know that she appears to be sleeping. Granted, her vital signs -- blood pressure, temperature, and pulse -- are normal. But there is more to life than that. Even if she opened her eyes, she could not see or do anything. She has had a massive stroke. There can be no recovery from that. You would be placing her in a situation where she could not talk or respond to you, would be unable to eat, and would need someone to wash her, change her clothes, and reposition her on the bed frequently. It is better to take her off the ventilator."

"Noooooooo," I wailed. "You are trying to kill my Momma!"

Junior took me outside and down to the end of the hall so we could talk and said, "The doctor knows these sorts of things, and we have to listen to him."

I continued to cry and scream no. Junior then told me that if we allowed the doctor to stop the ventilator and Momma even exhaled, he would beat that doctor to within an inch of his life.

It's amazing that voiced threats from my older siblings to do bodily harm to someone outside our family seemed to help alleviate bad situations for me. My sister Squeaky had made a similar threat when I was transferring to another elementary school and had heard that the teachers threw the children against the wall. At that time, she too promised to beat the teacher if she even thought of trying to do that to me. As they had when I was a child, my brother's words calmed me. I agreed to go back into Momma's room and watch them turn the life-giving machine off.

Momma did not move or exhale. Life as I knew it, ceased to exist.

Sadness has a way of hardening the heart and soul as it seeps into the crevices of one's being. For me, it was a constant companion. Promiscuity, partying, and late nights were the salves that I sought to ease my floundering sense of loss. I now began skipping all my early morning classes, resulting in mediocre and failing grades. Young college boys appear to sense when girls are at their most vulnerable point. A girl from the ghetto, such as I was, could easily be swayed by the trappings of wealth when her brain circuitry was haywire. Such was the case when Val came calling in his convertible sports car. After a few expensive restaurant dates and visits to his lavish apartment, I was wooed into a sexual liaison with him.

Even from the grave, mothers have a way of reaching out to pull children back before they go so far that they are at the point of no return. One night Momma came to me in a dream saying, "Baby, you are making yourself sick. I'm here with Big Momma, Rosie (my momma's sister), and Aunt Rosie (Big Momma's sister). We are all fine. Let that smile come back to your face. Start working on the things we talked about."

That morning when I awakened, I heard the birds singing for the first time since Momma had died. Val and his sports car no longer cast their allure. I became as involved in college as I had been in high school. No, I couldn't be a part of the marching band nor any of the dance clubs. It appeared that these college kids had always had dance and music lessons before they arrived in college. As previous majorettes, they all knew how to twirl batons and play instruments. I knew neither! Therefore, I turned my attention to other campus organizations in which I could become active.

1967 – President Johnson appoints Thurgood Marshall as the first Black Supreme Court Justice. The United States Supreme Court rules that prohibiting interracial marriage is unconstitutional, and sixteen states have to revise their anti-miscegenation laws.

12 - EXCHANGE PROGRAM IN GERMANY

Summer, 1967 – Racial tensions are increasing across the United States. Riots break out in Watts, Detroit, and Washington, D.C. Black rioters loot and burn businesses, including those owned by Blacks.

During my junior year of college, I was selected to participate in an international student exchange program, which sent students to live in other countries for a summer. I was a German major with a political science minor. In my studies, I had read many of the great works of German literature by Goethe and others, as well as everything possible about Hitler's Germany and World War II. So, I chose to travel to Germany. Not only was this an opportunity to visit another country and interact with German students in their homes, but I also had the opportunity to travel to New York City.

New York was the meeting place for all the American students who had been selected to participate in the exchange program. There were ten Americans in our Germany-bound group, including our Mormon leader. Of the nine students, Gladys, from Missouri, and I hit it off almost immediately. We were a matched pair as we toured New York City for those few days prior to boarding the ship. I told her about my experiences in Chicago during high school, and she enlightened me on the marvels of St. Louis. The skyscrapers in Chicago and the structures in St. Louis were nothing compared to what we saw in New York! I personally thought that New York City must have had the tallest buildings, widest streets, and most insane drivers in the world. I saw one driver cross three lanes of traffic and make a left turn from the farthest right lane; I was more than ready to leave New York.

Departure day arrived, and we boarded a small Italian ship, which had as its destination, Le Havre, France. Stormy seas tossed our little boat and its inhabitants from one side of the boat to the other. Meal times were not meant to be enjoyed under such conditions. I could only stay upright in a sitting or standing position for twenty minutes before the urge to bring up everything but my toes engulfed me those first three days. Finally the storm passed, and we were able to enjoy our transatlantic voyage. Having learned to play bridge in college, I was able to find games with some of the old-lady passengers to entertain myself.

There were three Negroes (we were no longer called "Colored" at this time; in some circles we were now called Blacks) on the ship -- an older man with his ten-year-old son, and me. Other than a smiling nod, we never interacted with each other. In retrospect, I wish that I had at least asked their names, where they were from, and where they were going. Though we were essentially isolated from others on the ship, I at least had my exchange-student mates to share the ongoing adventure. A costume contest was slated for the fourth night out, and my group decided that we should enter it to have a chance at winning the bottle of champagne listed as the prize. We decided to make an M-and-M cardboard costume and place it over my head! On the night of the contest, the announcer introduced the next entrant, "Plain Chocolate Candy!" Out I stepped. The audience roared with laughter. We were certain that first place was a lock for us and were ready for our bottle of champagne. Unfortunately, our prize was just a box of chocolates! We wondered if our leader had anything to do with the prize change?!

When we arrived at the port in Le Havre, France, there were many expectant people and noisy animals lining the boardwalk of the harbor. Gladys and I looked at each other and said almost simultaneously, "I wonder if the dogs are barking in French?"

Everything about this arrival was exciting, from ship disembarkation to embarkation on the trains which would take us to Germany. Italian, French, English, and German were but a few of the languages that were being used on our train by the students who were en route to these various countries. Vacationers who had either the good fortune (or terrible misfortune!) of traveling with a bunch of rowdy college students were also among the travelers.

As the train pulled into the station at Aachen, Germany, we saw this smiling man waiting to board; he was sporting a Stetson hat and cowboy boots. This dashing figure would turn out to be none other than our German leader and my "brother," Bernd. He wanted to be with us when we first set foot on German soil prior to our arrival in our homestay city of Bonn. In Bonn, at the Bahnhof, our German families waited for us. They stood at the train station expectantly waving American flags, shouting out greetings, laughing, snapping pictures, and trying to ascertain who was who!

We were all finally dispatched to the appropriate family hosts and left the train station. It was my twenty-first birthday, and upon arrival at their home, we found that *Mutti* (Bernd's name for his mother and the way she was introduced to me) had prepared *erdbeeren kuchen* to celebrate my birthday. What a delightful surprise that strawberry-like cake was!

I opened my gifts, ate my *erdbeeren kuchen*, and went for a walk along the Rhine River with Bernd. As we strolled back to the house, I mused on what Momma would be feeling if she could share this experience with me. I was certain that overseas travel had never entered her conscious mind. It was 9:00 p.m. when we entered the house and found that everyone had gone to bed for the night. I went to my room and, for the third time in my life, had an overwhelming sense of loneliness, which brought a deluge of tears. This time, there would be no Uncle Ed to remind me of Daddy and bring a modicum of comfort. Fortunately, my body responded to the day's travel and excitement, and I fell asleep very quickly.

Bernd, an art major, had to finish up some studies at a school outside of Bonn during my first few days there, so I was left to my own devices to explore and entertain myself. At the end of my first week, Bernd invited me to visit him at his art school so that I could see another neighboring town. Little did I know that he was going to use this as an avenue to try to lure me into a sexual liaison! He didn't realize that I had been brought up in the 'hood and had recently failed one test in "smooth talk" from a guy. Momma's voice in my head brought me back from the brink then, and now I would not make the same mistake twice! His orchestrated, "smooth" moves were too rough around the edges for me to succumb to him anyway, and I quickly arranged to get the next train back to Bonn! Having reached the ripe old age of twenty-one, I was able to move forward without internal blame, which would have been another notch on my belt of insecurities.

Even though everyone rode bicycles, I took excursions into town by bus. It was while I was waiting for the bus on one of these excursions that I met my young German protectors, Alfreeda, Hans, and Gregor. They began speaking to me and quickly realized that I was not very good with the spoken German language. It was fascinating to them that I was grown up and could not speak as well as they could! In every city in the world, there are bullies, and Bonn was no different. A group of boys rode up on their bikes, and upon seeing my dark skin, started taunting me. Alfreeda and crew threw rocks and stones at them to shoo them away from their very own personal *"Negerin"*! My "Protectors" managed to arrive within minutes of my appearance each day, with sticks and stones in hand, just in case the need arose for them to run off the bullies. They were also eager to help me learn to speak German better. Each day, after our short social time at the bus stop, I safely made my trek to discover more about Bonn.

To vary my routine, my *Mutti* took me on a visit to the home of one of her friends, where I experienced my first taste of Schnapps! Wow, did that sting and burn as it made its fiery way down my throat. *Mutti's* friend had a daughter who was an avid hiker, and we were given the opportunity to hike up into the *Sieben Geburge*, the mountains on the outskirts of Bonn. My *Papi*, Bernd's father, was a newspaper man, who interviewed me after this adventure. The one outstanding feature in the resulting article was my continuing complaint of the *muskelkrampfe* ("Charlie horses") in my calves that attacked me after my mountain climbing adventure!

Our group spent the first two weeks in Bonn and met with various government officials, including the mayor and members of the German chancellery. We each then took one member of our German family and departed on a bus tour of Germany, Switzerland, and Austria. Ironically, my family member, Bernd, was also the "adult leader" of the German students. As I had already experienced, "leaders" were not always true to the high standards of the exchange organization. I chose to put his inappropriate behavior behind me so that I could take full advantage of this experience.

This six-week bus journey had many memorable and fun moments, which included a visit to the famous Hofbrau House in

Munich, artistic masterpiece viewings, a climb and several-night stay in the Swiss Alps, chance encounters with other American tourists, an overnight stay in the home of a probable Nazi, and a visit to East Berlin.

My German "brother," the art major, made certain that we saw every church in Germany and the art contained therein! They all had a cemetery associated with them. Those visits afforded me my first opportunity to see a Nazi swastika up close and personal, since they were engraved on many headstones.

On our stop at the Hofbrau House in Munich, we sang and drank the night away with all of the other tourists and Germans. When we returned to the youth hostel, Gladys was so wasted that she peed in the closet, which she mistook for a bathroom!

Our travels took us to the German side of the Swiss Alps, a magnificent marvel of creation. Our bus parked in the valley, and we had the chore of hiking two-miles up a steep incline to reach the cabin in which we would stay. At one point, I could only see mountain dirt in my face and a sheer drop behind me! I swore to Bernd that if I ever got down, I would never make that climb again in life. Upon arriving at the cabin and viewing yet even more majestic Alps all around me, that thought was quickly dispelled. It was so neat to appear to be in yet another valley, while knowing that we had climbed up from a previous valley! We saw snow falling atop the mountains surrounding us, while the sun was shining on our level in the valley. At night, we sat around camp fires and cooked food, some in tin cans, on an open fire. Though my momma used tin pots on top of our wood-fired iron stove, this experience was somewhat reminiscent of my childhood. This made the time even more fun in this new world of exploration and experimentation.

After our time was up for this stop, we packed our bags, hiked back down to the valley below, and hopped on our big blue bus. Our journey was now set for Salzburg, Austria.

Upon arrival in Salzburg, we stayed in a youth hostel on a mountain across from the one where *The Sound of Music* was filmed. Though I had never seen this movie, it was interesting to note that I was close to an American movie scene. By this juncture in our trip, we Americans were all fluent in German. We decided to have dinner at a tiny restaurant and bar, which was built into the side of a mountain at the bottom of the one where our youth hostel was located. When we got there, we came upon a group of rowdy Americans from Texas. The Americans in our group pretended not to understand English. Our German cohorts would translate into German the things that the Americans were saying, and we would ask questions in German for them to translate into English! It was great fun putting this over on the visiting group of Americans. They bought us drinks, and everybody was lit! Again, Gladys drank so much that she could not walk straight; Bernd, in his inebriated state, picked her up and threw her over his shoulder to get her back up to the cabin. The next day he didn't understand why his legs ached so!

The saying "small world" was vividly portrayed to me on an outing to window-shop in downtown Salzburg. Having seen no other people of color during my stay in Europe thus far, I did a double-take when a brown form materialized in the corner of my eye as we passed an entrance to a department store. As I backed up, I realized that it was Thomas, another Howard University student who was on an exchange program to Austria. We screamed and started hugging each other and talking at the same time, as though we were long lost relatives! In retrospect, it was amazing that the police weren't called. At home, we often heard that "the presence of two Blacks in one place could signal the onset of a riot!"

When we arrived in Switzerland, we were assigned in groups of three or four, to sleep in private homes. I had already had an inkling of how Blacks were perceived over there from pictures that had been displayed in a famous library. There was a large book under a secure glass whose page was turned to a depiction of a Black American G. I. who had a tail affixed to his bottom, as though he were a member of a monkey family! Armed with this knowledge and my growing German fluency, I became an Italian student traveling with this group of Americans!

My group was assigned to the home of a man that we decided was a former Nazi! His conversation at dinner was all derogatory about the "*Negerin*" in Detroit who were rioting and burning down the city. He said that they should have been treated like the Jews had been treated during the war! I made sure that my German was pitch-perfect at that time! I could not wait for the morning to come so that I could get out of there before he realized that I was not an Italian student. Fortunately for me, he could not speak Italian!

Our last stop in Germany took us to West Berlin, which at the time was still a part of East Germany. The Berlin Wall was still in existence, and there was a decidedly different East vs. West mentality. Guards patrolling the walls were not supposed to communicate with anyone on the West Berlin side of the wall. Of course Gladys and I were determined to change that! We did can-can dances and raised our skirts to them! They responded by placing their hands down on the West Berlin side and waving. When any West Berlin police approached, we immediately began looking for something in the grass!

We had to cross Checkpoint Charlie in order to go into East Berlin and were given the "no photography and no fraternization" rules before our trip over. Rebellious youth that I was, I could not abide that! I constantly held my camera at my side so that I could secretly snap and photograph Russian troop-transports and soldiers undetected! Had I been caught, I probably would still have been over there when the Berlin wall came down! It was fascinating to see the East Berlin museums that had life-sized replicas of bombed-out buildings, homes, and life as it had been during the war.

West Berlin also had its standing memorabilia of the war in the buildings that had been bombed but not torn down, as a reminder of how it had been during the war. What a contrast this afforded from the modern new infrastructure that had been built after the war. We were also treated to an opera in the newly rebuilt West Berlin opera house. Having been exposed only to rhythm-and-blues, this was yet another fascinating experience for me.

Our last stop in Europe prior to returning to the United States occurred in Paris, where we were housed in a regular hotel as opposed to the youth hostels in Germany and Austria. A couple of our German friends bicycled to Paris to meet us, where they were able to sneak into our rooms at the hotel. There was such a great anti-American sentiment at that time that we all chose to speak German when we were in public rather than risk being labeled "ugly Americans"!

What an adventure we had!

13 - BACK TO COLLEGE FOR SENIOR YEAR

Returning to school after such an exciting time could have been a major letdown had it not been for the expectation of graduation at the end of the year. Unfortunately, this was not to be a smooth year.

April 4, 1968 – Martin Luther King is assassinated in Memphis, Tennessee.

April 11, 1968 – President Johnson signs the Civil Rights Act of 1968, which prohibited discrimination in the sale, rental, and financing of housing.

Assassinations, political unrest in the country, and unrest on our college campus put into question whether I would actually graduate in May! In the spring, we took over the "A" building (administration building) of Howard University to make them acquiesce to our student demands! As I lay dozing on the cold concrete floor and thought about eating either spaghetti or hot dogs the next day, I didn't feel that I would ever be able to graduate. In spite of all of the civil unrest going on in the country, this was the very first time that I had decided to leave my comfort zone and be a part of the change! It had taken me a while to accept the beauty of our first Afro-wearing homecoming queen! Though I had missed several opportunities to hear some of our more preeminent social-change advocates – Stokeley Carmichael and H. Rap Brown – my social-consciousness meter was finally beginning to peek out of its shell.

During this sit-in, we allowed only one Black journalist into the building to cover our actions. We were front page news for several days, and my backside was rapidly growing tired of this hard, cold existence. Fortunately, an agreement was reached, and the "A" building was turned back over to the university officials.

I was eager to share the excitement with my family back home and give voice to my "Black Pride/Black Power" stance. Unfortunately, Squeaky quickly shot me down from my headiness!

"Momma didn't send you up there to get involved in 'all of that craziness.' You only have a few months to go before you can finish college and come home. Don't get involved in any more rallies!" There has always been something about invoking the name of "Momma" to make me back up and toe the line! I decided to steer clear of any further rallies.

End-of-school exams and upcoming graduation preparation saw a flurry of activity. Everyone was making the trip to see me graduate from college – the first one in the family to do so. Four of my siblings -- Vern, Gert, Boe, and Jobie -- drove up to Washington, D.C., along with my daddy. My sister Squeaky was in a tuberculosis hospital and could not come. My brother Junior stayed behind so that she would have someone there if she needed anything.

The campus of Howard University was abuzz with excitement and activity in preparation for the upcoming graduation ceremony. My family contingent from Smokey City made themselves an integral part of any activity they saw. Sororities and fraternities were putting on "step shows," and everyone was enjoying the shows and snapping pictures.

"Say Cheese!" seemed to be the new phrase for the weekend.

Everyone on campus could be seen in various poses, "cheesing" in front of someone's camera. The day of the graduation ceremony was no different.

It's amazing that there was room on the campus for anyone else because my family's chests were so big with pride that they were close to exploding! Their baby girl from Smokey City was to be the very first person in the family to receive a college degree! The celebration continued into the night but had to be cut short so that they could get on the road and make the long drive back to Memphis.

I had been interviewed for and offered a job as a computer-programmer trainee at the MCC Corporation. I was now preparing to move from the dorm into my first apartment.

14 - FIRST JOB AFTER COLLEGE

I had a two-month break before my job started. I had also found a part-time job working in downtown Washington, D.C. to support myself until I started with MCC. I remember being advised to invest some money in a small upstart company called Xerox by one of the managers in the office. I also remember saying thanks, but no thanks! I needed all of my earnings to live on and help set up my new apartment.

Aaah, youth!

Learning binary code and assembly language was relatively simple for me at that time, and I successfully completed the training program. At its conclusion, I was offered and accepted a full-time position as a programmer, earning $8,232.00 per year. I thought I was close to being rich! As I progressed, I had the opportunity to work on one of the space missions at NASA. It was a small but integral part of the mission. It was during this time that I took vacation and made a road trip to upstate New York with my old roommate, Sarita. The voiced reason for the trip was to visit our friend, Joanne, and her family, but we really wanted to experience the nightlife of New York!

Buffalo was the least happening city in the world! Everything was closed by 9:00 p.m.! This would not do for recent college grads who had their very own money in their pockets for the first time in life! Both of us were from the South, she from North Carolina and I from Tennessee. Therefore, when Joanne invited us up to New York, visions of bright lights and partying came to mind! Sadly this was not to be. We had to make tracks from there without insulting Joanne's parents. We made up this elaborate story that the satellite mission I was working on was on the verge of losing its orbit! I had to go back and reprogram the docking section of the software! With that lie convincingly told, we got up early the next morning and hit the road back to D.C. to finish our short vacation.

At the time, I didn't know that Sarita had been approached by this tall, dark, and handsome chocolate law student who was interested in me and my beautiful legs! She took this opportunity to call him and let him know that we would be in town together for the rest of the weekend. Little did I know that I was being introduced to my future husband, Moses Hunter, III.

He was a photography buff, who dreamed of placing his work on the cover of Life magazine. He even had his own darkroom, which was quite intriguing to me! The only camera I had ever seen was a Kodak Brownie at school, and there was no accompanying darkroom, at least to my knowledge. Photographs in my home were practically nonexistent, even though my daddy would always say when I was dressed up that we should take a picture! Moses and I often went down to Haines Point, where he would photograph me, and invariably my legs would play a prominent role in these photographs.

After one such sojourn, I decided to venture into his darkroom on my own to see how the pictures had turned out. "Inquisitive Me" wanted to see everything first, and my pawing around in the darkroom for a light switch was fortuitous for Moses. He heard me and was able to stop the light from coming on, which I then found out would have destroyed all of his negatives! He later introduced this part of his world to me without the presence of film negatives.

As we became acquainted with each other, I learned that he was also a gun enthusiast and sports car buff. All of this was new to me, primarily due to my lack of exposure to such things. The only thing I knew about guns was that the "Saturday Night Special" was the weapon of choice when knives failed at the Bier Garten in my old neighborhood! Prior to high school, the only car that we owned was a used Model-T Ford, which could only be started occasionally. I realized that growing up in an economically deprived family did not allow for such frivolities as cameras, guns, and sports cars.

Our backgrounds could not have been farther apart. His parents were both college educated, with careers as a principal and a pharmacist. My dad finished third grade prior to 1920, and my mom finished eighth grade prior to 1925. Though I gave lip service to being interested in his hobbies, I never fully gained an appreciation nor interest in any of them. What was of interest to me was the fact that he was going to become a Lawyer!

No one in my family had ever dated a lawyer, doctor, or Indian-chief type! My momma's famous last words were always, "It is just as easy to love and marry a rich man as it is a poor one!" Even though marriage was not in mind for the near future, "lawyer" automatically meant enhanced economic status, if that were to become a possibility!

After several months of dating, he asked me to marry him, and it came as a complete shock to me. I was flabbergasted and didn't know what to say. Marriage was the farthest thing from my mind. Being the lawyer and persuasive talker, he convinced me that this was the perfect time for us to get married. After staying up half the night with this conversation, I agreed to marry him. We planned to go to the Eastern Shore the next weekend for him to introduce me to his parents. Walking into Mrs. Hunter's house made my hair stand on end. Little did I know that I may have been the Antichrist as far as she was concerned! His father, on the other hand was one of the sweetest men that I had ever met; ours was not to be a long acquaintance because he died the next spring, before Moses and I were married.

Mrs. Hunter was determined to thwart our marriage plans and hired an investigator to dig up dirt on me to use as ammunition in her fight against this union. The only thing the man could find was that I had been brought up in abject poverty. A wife from such meager beginnings, college educated or not, was totally unacceptable for her only son.

Fortunately, he was not swayed by her negativism and proceeded on with plans to marry me.

15 - MARRIAGE AND ITS DISSOLUTION

Even though I returned to her house as her only son's wife, I was still given the very cold shoulder and made to feel very unwelcome in her home. Fortunately, I didn't have to make frequent trips to visit. Our daughter, Eriell, was born a year and a half after we were married. After her birth, it was decided that I should stay home and be a full-time mother. Eriell had other plans for me and quickly outgrew the need for my constant attention! My days were not filled with anything other than my child, so I had to find other outlets that would still allow me to spend the lion's share of my time with my daughter while guiding her development. I sold real estate and taught computer programming, neither of which was very rewarding. At the same time, all romance seemed to have left my marriage and my husband, and we coexisted as good roommates. So here I was, with few outside interests and a ho-hum marriage that was rapidly going nowhere! I began musing about the possibility of one of my childhood thoughts of becoming a doctor.

I went to Howard and inquired about the coursework that I would need, since I had never taken any of the science courses in undergraduate school. My investigation showed me that I would have to take the physics labs in another year because I would not have the time to get all of the biology, chemistries (inorganic and organic) and their labs, plus physics and its lab in one year. I decided to move forward and take the prerequisites for med school over the next two years and determine if the sciences really did interest me. To my surprise, I was pumped up and made a game out of it with one of my professors. His challenge was that his exams would be too difficult for me to make an A on them. I took it one step farther and said that I would make a perfect score on his exams! And I did! I thoroughly enjoyed taking the pre-med requirements over those two years. I knew that a career in medicine was the correct move for me to make at that time.

The next hurdle was getting admitted to medical school. The only schools in the area that I considered were Howard University College of Medicine and the University of Maryland medical school. At Maryland, I was not only accepted but also given a scholarship for the first year, which would be renewable in subsequent years based upon my performance. Howard, on the other hand, had not even granted me an interview!

Into this dilemma walked my friend, Ronaldo from undergraduate school, who knew some assistant deans at Howard. He introduced us and told me that I was responsible for convincing them that I would make a good student. Later, I interviewed with Marilyn Lang, Dean of Admissions. She expressed some concern about my advanced age, (29 when school would start), motherhood and how those factors would impact my ability to handle the course work required of medical students. I assured her that I was prepared and that I had a good support system in place. My responses were obviously satisfactory and I received my acceptance letter to Howard University College of Medicine a few days later. My excitement after I was accepted at Howard was palpable! I could not believe that this little Smokey City girl was on her way and had taken the first step toward becoming a doctor!

16 - MEDICAL SCHOOL

During the summer before medical school started, I attended a preparatory course intended to help older students and those who had not done well in the sciences during undergraduate school. Part of this prep included viewing and touching previously dissected bodies in the anatomy lab as the last session before lunch. The Wonder Bread Bakery was just around the corner from the medical school. The aromas of freshly baked bread wafted through the open window of the anatomy lab as though they were come-hither fingers of a temptress. The Florida Ave Grill, across the street from the bakery, added its lingering smell of fried chicken. With the compelling aromas of bread and chicken, the speed of observation of anatomical parts picked up drastically. The goal was now to get across the street and feed the hungry beast that my stomach had become. Having worked in the office across the street part-time for the past two years, I was well acquainted with the meals available at the Florida Ave Grill.

I was finally able to leave the anatomy lab and found the day outside to be smolderingly hot. After ordering and receiving my chicken breast straight out of the grease, I bit into it. The chicken wasn't quite as tasty as it usually was with that first bite. Had Mr. Beasley hired a new cook in the kitchen, I mused.

For southern fried chicken to be right, it needed the exact amount of salt and pepper before it was battered and lowered into the piping hot grease. When chicken and grease connected, pops of hot grease would splatter far and wide if the cold meat was placed in the grease too quickly. The grease, of course, had its own seasoning from the many pieces of chicken that had crackled, popped, and browned in it on previous days. I tried a couple of other bites, but visions of dead, stringy bodies overtook my senses, forcing me to throw my chicken away! It was a full six weeks into the first fall of medical school before I could eat chicken or any other meat again! Eventually, I could dissect a body with one hand while holding a chicken thigh in the other.

Many adaptations had to occur with my new life as a budding young doctor.

It was here that my marriage would undergo its major testing ground. My husband was constantly being warned that he would waste his money and time on me, because as soon as I finished medical school, I would leave him! I heard this first hand when he left the phone off the hook, and I heard a female voice saying those very words.

"She is using you and will leave you as soon as she finishes school. You should come and move in with me now."

At another stage of my marriage, I would have been furious to hear such a thing! But instead of making an issue of what I had heard, I turned on a television program which was discussing, of all things, the future of marriage in this country!

When Moses came into the room and sat for a few minutes, I turned to him and said, "Speaking of marriage, where do you think ours is headed?"

After a few moments of silent thought, he turned to me and said, "Well you know Ruth, it seems to be going nowhere fast."

I then responded, "Perhaps we should consider separating for a while."

After a few minutes spent pondering my statement, he said "Okay, I will look into getting a place soon."

He obviously had already bought into the things his "lady friend" had said and felt that this would be an opportune time to begin the dissolution of our marriage. In March of my freshman year in medical school, he left me and our daughter and moved into an apartment in D.C. This would be the first of several challenges that I would have to overcome as a single mother who was also a medical student. He let it be known that he would not be available to babysit our then- three-year-old daughter, and that I would have to find someone to care for her while I was at school or needed to be away from home. Never having been one to grovel at anyone's feet, I knew that I would find the means to handle this minor bump in my wheel of progress. Fortune smiled on me, and Mrs. Thurston, whose son I had dated in college, introduced me to Mrs. Danville, who turned out to be a Godsend. Her house was located approximately three miles from the medical school and was in a direct path for me as I drove to D.C. from Maryland. She prepared breakfast, lunch, and sometimes dinner for Eriela. She also taught her table manners.

Occasionally, I had to take Eriela to the medical school with me in the evening for anatomy lab work. I remembered the day that we sat in the back of the auditorium, and I was learning the chambers of the heart. To my amazement, Eriela had been learning them, too. When I incorrectly named one of the chambers a ventricle, my three-year-old said, "No mommy, that's the atrium"! (What a lightning bolt of clarity about little ones' natural capacity to soak up information in and from their environment struck me in that moment.)

I was fortunate enough to develop a wonderful study group: Michelle, Mitchell, and Dwayne. Whenever the need arose, they would take turns watching Eriela at the school or coming to my house so that I did not have to study alone.

The enormity of the textbooks, with their millions of pieces of information that students were required to learn, was daunting. The first two years primarily involved the textbooks and learning the science. January of my second year was going to be another huge hurdle, as I took the all-encompassing neuroscience course, which covered the anatomy, physiology, biochemistry, and pharmacology of the nervous system. My sister Gert came to my rescue and offered to keep Eriela for that month back in my hometown. We packed and prepared for our sojourn down south on the train. Unlike the speedy, clean trains I had been exposed to in Europe, this one pulled up at every whistle-stop between D.C. and Tennessee. If that was not enough, it also had a couple of mechanical breakdowns that caused three-hour delays. Fortunately, my sweet baby girl slept through much of this adventure and was quite awake and excited when we finally pulled into the train station in Memphis. I, on the other hand, was totally exhausted and immediately began lamenting the fact that I would have to make a return trip so soon on that broken-down steel to get back to school. Within a few hours, another blessing dropped in my lap. My friend Sarita had opened her own marketing firm and, after hearing of my saga, offered to fund my airfare back to school. After getting Eriela settled in for her month-long visit at my sister's house, I left the next morning and headed back to D.C.

After I finished the neuroscience course, I got a peek into the future with a course called "Patients, Doctors, and Society." I and my fellow students actually had a chance to learn how to conduct patient examinations and take medical histories using real people! Although they were actors, these people were well versed in the disease process that they supposedly had. It was here that I heard and really learned about vital signs, the key to all patient examinations. As with most of my goals, I was anxious to get to the end and become a doctor.

The last two years of medical school were that portal into the future, the clinical years of learning patient evaluations and management. Whether seeing patients in the clinic or in their hospital rooms, this was an exciting and mind-expanding time. There were many opportunities for lessons to be reinforced. During a coronary care rotation, I passed by the window of a patient's room and noticed that the monitor above his bed was showing a flat line! I pushed the button to activate "Dr. Dan," the code words broadcasting the necessity for immediate resuscitation of a patient whose heart had stopped. I then summoned all of my forces to administer a huge pre-cordial thump with my fist on the chest of this very large man.

He opened his eyes widely and screamed, "Why are you beating me?"

To my dismay, I had bypassed the routine of assessment of vital signs and looked only at a cardiac monitor with a disconnected lead. Thus, a flat lined EKG! That was a major learning experience that would remain with me, forever.

On those occasions where a Dr. Dan was called and needed, I learned the ABCs of assessment and resuscitation of patients.

1978 – The United States Supreme Court upholds the constitutionality of affirmative action in the Regents of the University of California v. Bakke.

17 - DADDY – MAY, 1979

The week before I was to graduate from medical school, my dad had a stroke. Though my family tried to downplay the severity of it, I had the need to talk to Daddy directly. I was always very intuitive and listened to my instincts. Upon hearing his voice, I decided to fly home immediately.

After I arrived in Memphis, my sister Squeaky and I went directly to the hospital from the airport. Daddy was asleep and groggily opened his eyes to acknowledge my presence, but he promptly fell back into a deep sleep, as demonstrated by his deep sonorous breathing. I would be receiving my MD in a few days and therefore felt empowered to evaluate my dad's medical care by reviewing his medical chart.

Squeaky screamed, "Ruth, Daddy's eyes are rolling back in his head."

I took charge.

My brain went into overdrive as I gave instructions to Squeaky to call the family and told the nurse to call the code team. To myself, I revived the life-giving Dr. Dan routine from medical school. "Ruth, start chest compressions! Breathe for your daddy! Force his vital signs to return!"

After the arrival of the code team, I left my daddy, with cardiac resuscitation in progress. While I was walking down the hall, my chest began rebelling again. Surely, God was not going to allow a stroke to take yet another parent.

Daddy survived that night but remained comatose for two

months. He awakened one day when Gert was preparing to clean him up and said, "Hey Lady, I'm hungry as a wolf!"

This was yet another lesson for me; I never gave up on my patients. Daddy had many more years of life left in him before he died in his sleep at age ninety-four.

18 - JARRETT

Not only had medical school become a plethora of exciting science and patient-care activities, it had been a meeting place for new and interesting friends. Every Friday night, on the top floor of the medical school, students would arrive for "The Doctors' Stop." Music would be blaring and bodies would be shaking all over the dance floor. Several relationships blossomed under the heat and rhythm that raced through the minds of these young scholars who were releasing the pent up stresses and nervous energy that had consumed them during the previous week. My best buds -- my study group Michelle, Dwayne, and Mitchell -- were always there and sweating to the beat of the "oldies but goodies."

Standing on the periphery was a quiet, gray-eyed young brother from Texas. He never danced and seemed to always be alone.

One evening, I, in my effervescent bubbly way said, "Hi sweetie, let me see you make some moves." He turned me down with a shy smile. Never one to take no for an answer, I persisted and within a month, I had him at least slow dancing on the floor. Shortly thereafter, he joined our fearsome foursome study group. It soon became apparent to all of us that "Mr. Quiet" was also "Mr. Brilliant"! He quickly left us all in the dust academically and was able to finish medical school in three years instead of the usual four! "Mr. Brilliant," or Jarret as his parents called him, took more than a passing interest in me. Though I wanted to engage him in the party happenings, I never dreamed of any relationship beyond that. One huge negative in my mind was his age. He was seven years younger than I was at the time! I would occasionally try to fix him up with other young ladies. Fortunately for me, he would periodically come back and try to forge a relationship with me. After several months of this, I stopped trying to fix him up, and we became an item!

On many days, he could be seen sitting under one of the trees in front of the school, penning some lovely prose to give to me. I had never felt so special to anyone in my life! After his graduation and during my senior year, he asked me to marry him, and so we did!

Decisions needed to be made during the last year of medical school as to which specialty I wanted to pursue. My plan was to become a surgeon, so I began my training as a surgery intern. I vacillated between general surgery and urology as a specialty. I applied and was accepted as the first woman into the urology program at Howard. At the same time, I heard that another woman had just been accepted into the urology program at Walter Reed Army Hospital as most people called it then. My lack of self-confidence took control. I felt that I could not compete with another female in the same specialty, finishing at the same time! I still had not grown enough to realize that the United States was a big place! In addition, I knew that urology required two years of general surgery. General surgery was definitely out because I learned that surgery residents needed to travel for several months out of the year to Alabama and Ohio. I had no intention of being without my family for such long periods! Those were sufficient reasons; I did a 180-degree turn and decided to become an anesthesiologist.

Jarrett was well into his internal medicine training before I began my anesthesiology training. We both were eager to add to our family and elected to do so during our residencies. Though he would finish his internal medicine before I would finish anesthesiology, we decided that he should wait in D.C. with me, and then we would go off together to do fellowships. With both of us training at Howard Hospital, we often ran into each other in the hallway or elevator and were able to sneak a quick kiss or hug during the day!

Jarrett was also busy with his residency group, preparing to take the internal medicine boards. At that time, our "beepers" could be used as voice phones. It was during one of his study sessions that I paged and sang out loudly to the room, "Jarrett, you're going to be a daddy!" Though a joyous announcement, it was slightly embarrassing for Jarrett to have everyone in the room to hear it at the same time as he! Oh well, that was his Ruth, he smiled to himself.

As surgery interns, my team was constantly climbing flights of stairs while on patient rounds. My pregnancy and enormous weight gain made these treks a bit precarious. My attending physician finally said, "I haven't delivered a baby in twenty years, so you must take the elevator!"

My fingers became so swollen that I could no longer take off my wedding rings. This rapidly curtailed my ability to scrub in on surgeries. The cafeteria workers were constantly loading my plate with food – two meats, three vegetables, two desserts, and lemonade!

"Honey, you are eating for two," was the refrain I heard any time that I was in the lunch or dinner line. I never was successful at saying no. Two weeks before our baby was born, I weighed a whopping 192 pounds!

Delivery time brought about the curse of being a medical professional. The epidural for my C-section was not working. As my lips began to tingle and the room became fuzzy, I heard the anesthesiologist say, "I have to put her to sleep. I've given her more than enough and it still is not giving her a complete block." I remembered crying out in a muffled sound, "Noooooo!" I was told later by Jarret that one single tear hung at the corner of my eye as I was plunged rapidly into darkness.

Jarrett was not without incident either because as they tugged and pulled on the baby's head, he nearly fainted thinking they were going to pull his baby's head off! Fortunately, an astute nurse slid a stool under him as she saw him become unbalanced!

I awakened to the sounds of suction catheters and voices, one of which was saying, "Take a deep breath."

It took a few moments for it to register where I was and then ask, "What did we have?"

Jarrett said, "A girl, and her feet are fat and flat like mine. Even her little toe looks just like mine!" Jarrett and I had often laughed about his malformed right little toe. Since the nail was turned to the side, we decided that this toe was an afterthought by God! He had looked down and seen that there were not five, so He threw a glob on the side of Jarrett's foot to complete the set!

I drifted in and out of sleep, asking the same question over and over: "What did we have?"

Six weeks was not nearly enough time for a new Mommy to spend with her new baby, Jai, but such was the life of a resident. I was fortunate to have been able to find relatives of friends to help with child care responsibilities while I trained to become a practicing anesthesiologist. Since Jarret had completed his internal medicine residency program, we had to decide how to proceed with further training. We agreed that the family unit would remain together. Jarret received permission to do one year of a cardiology fellowship at Howard while he waited for his wife to finish her anesthesiology training. He had already been accepted as a cardiology fellow at the Cardiac Center in Houston for the following year.

PART II – THE BASTION OF MALE SUPERIORITY

"Dr. C., he is beginning to decompensate," I say.

He looks up at me and barks loudly, "I have the aorta wide open! What do you expect me to do?!"

"Sew fast," I respond.

My brain, eyes, and hands kick into overdrive as I determine which medications and fluids should receive their marching orders.

"Get me another pair of hands in here," I scream to the nurse.

My resident is becoming paralyzed with his inexperience and moving slower as I speed up.

The Cell Saver tech has the machine going full out, processing the blood returning from the operative field and rushing back into the patient's large bore central catheter.

The heart stops beating. My last interchange with Mr. Jonah runs fleetingly across my brain.

"You pay me to wake you up!"

The surgeon gives three mighty squeezes to the heart, followed by intermittent suturing of the graft. This dance continues for several minutes. I continue to rapidly provide fluid and medications to normalize blood pressure and heart function. Their current values are threatening to put an irreversible death grip on this patient.

The brain waves are slowing to a crawl.

The surgeon and I are the only ones in flat-out, full-speed-ahead motion. Everyone else in the room seems to have gone into slow motion as they anticipate the end.

The last suture goes into the graft ...

19 - POST-GRADUATE TRAINING

The words "post-graduate" and "training" appear to be innocuous terms, on the surface. I was prepared to learn an advanced skill set to give me additional expertise in my chosen profession. What I was not prepared for was the constant barrage of minimizations to my character and intellect due to the color of my skin! The "professionals" that I encountered during my advanced training and subsequent career taught me how to manage my own personal civil rights movement!

Since my husband already had a fellowship position, it was now my turn to search for the same opportunity in Houston. I had already gained some facility with obstetric anesthesiology, but had little experience with cardiac anesthesiology. This, combined with Houston's reputation as a cardiac town, made me decide to search for a cardiac anesthesiology fellowship. My first stop was at the Cardiac Center. There, Chairman Kingsley invited me out to dinner. We dined at the then-famous Medico's Club, with its wood paneled decor, soft lighting cast by elegant chandeliers, and the melodious tunes played on the piano by Ray Vaughn.

The interview questions were the usual fare of background training, personal background, whys of interest in cardiac anesthesiology, and so on. Kingsley then launched into a description of his program as being one that catered to a very select group of surgeons. Their expertise, according to him, was far above any other in the world. Consequently, anesthetic techniques could not easily be transferred to other operating theaters around the country. I interjected that I had no interest in moving to other parts of the country and would be quite content to remain in Houston. After a few more pleasantries, dinner ended, and he told me that he "would be in touch."

My next stop on the interview trail took me to The City hospital district and Lance Lovington, director of residency training for the College of Medicine. Lance, a brusque, no-nonsense, rotund man, described the world of anesthesiology at their cardiac unit.

He said, "The surgeons are very difficult to work with, the hours are extremely long, and the anesthesiology staff is quite fragmented." After that illuminating introduction, he continued, "If you are still interested, I will send you over to speak with S. Rahn Rey, Chief of Cardiac Anesthesiology at The Private Hospital, where our residents receive their cardiac and thoracic training." Due to my naiveté about the inner workings of the "good ole boy" South, this warning fell on deaf ears.

The Private Hospital was one of the most prestigious hospitals in the area, and the only one connected to the College of Medicine. The hospital had built a suite of operating rooms to cater to the patients of two world-renowned surgeons, Dr. Maurice Dunkirk and Dr. Saul Levinsky. Dr. Levinsky was the master of the aorta, and Dr. Dunkirk was the master of all things cardiac, including the development of mechanical devices which could be used for the failing heart. These two had met during their surgical training and formed an unlikely alliance. Dr. Dunkirk was the son of the wealthy Dunkirk clan, whose textile manufacturing concerns had made them among the richest billionaires in the world. Dr. Levinsky, on the other hand, was the son of poor, first-generation immigrants who were still trying to make a fledgling corner grocery store successful enough to support them and their four children, of whom Saul was the oldest. Saul inherited his father's steadfast determination to succeed in life, and he was rewarded by being the only one in the family allowed to be educated in this country. The other three children were placed in the store and eventual cafeteria as workers to help the family business.

During their time in the lab as surgical residents, Maurice was continually trying to find a way for the heart to pump its blood in the face of damage from heart attacks. He constantly tinkered with devices that would provide external compressions while he witnessed the microscopic cell death of the rat hearts he was using. Saul, on the other hand, was fascinated with how blood circulated to the entire body. One evening, while discussing their mutual frustrations with their ongoing research projects, each had a sentinel moment occur while listening to the other!

Maurice said that he should have just stayed in the family business and sewn pencil skirts for girls. Saul visualized this "pencil" attire on extremely thin girls passing their table and said, "They look just like tubes! Blood runs through tubes in the body. What if we could make a fabric that would hold the blood in and connect it to damaged vessels in the body?"

This began in-earnest research that resulted in the formation of Dacron grafts, which were used to repair large blood vessels in the body. Saul continued his research and was able to come up with a novel approach to diseases of the aorta. His subsequent fame as "Master of the Aorta" worldwide was professionally lauded.

Maurice, in listening to Saul's musings, thought, "Why use manmade tubes to carry blood to the heart? It would be better to use some of the million miles of veins that are in the human body to be the transporters."

Despite many naysayers, he was successful in harvesting these veins and attaching them to the heart to bypass the blocked vessels which were causing heart muscle to die. He was able to visualize the return of life to damaged heart muscle that had died under similar circumstances in the past. These two singular efforts took cardiovascular surgery expectations into the stratosphere and made the doctors internationally famous for their work. With fame comes fortune, and their reputations grew. Not only were their services requested internationally, but they became magnets for research dollars. The College of Medicine quickly offered them full professorships and as much research space as they needed. Grant money rained into the College from those interested in being on the ground floor of such phenomenal scientific achievement.

The Private Hospital was not to be outdone, and subsequently built the doctors their own operating theater. Naturally, would-be surgeons flocked to the surgical residency program of the College of Medicine, now firmly ensconced at The Private Hospital. Associates of these two innovators, along with various underlings, flew to the complex in astounding numbers. These new practices, piggybacked on the shoulders of such giants, also grew at phenomenal rates. The amount of money brought into The Private Hospital gave this surgical specialty a power heretofore unequaled by any other service. The cardiac surgeons were given carte blanche to operate in this continually expanding suite at any time of the day or night. An elixir of power permeated the air surrounding these surgeons, whose sense of entitlement was unparalleled in the universe! Exposure to such headiness was not even in my conscious sphere of possibilities. I had no clue about what I might be facing, but I pressed on with the interview process.

I walked the few blocks to The Private Hospital and found my way into the cardiac unit. Upon entering the cardiac suite, I encountered F. Bissett, the nurse responsible for placing most of the peripheral intravenous and arterial catheters in the patients. I, with my Afro standing tall, went into the locker room to change clothes and walked up to the first African American face that I had seen, F. Bissett, to initiate a conversation.

"How is it around here?"

Mrs. Bissett, as she demanded that she be called, turned to me with an incredulous look and stated in this deep baritone voice, "You're Black, aren't you? What do you think?" Without another word, Mrs. Bissett turned abruptly and left me standing in the locker room with a very dismayed look on my face!

"Wow," I thought to myself, "What am in for if I stick around here!?"

After dressing, I went into the anesthesiology office, where Dr. S. Rahn Rey waited for me. Surprise, surprise, S. Rahn was a man! He was full of positive energy, and warmth exuded from him. As he described the life of an anesthesiology fellow to me, he tried to minimize the negativity that I had heard from Dr. Lovington.

He said, "Our weekdays do require long hours, but you will be free on weekends. We have several nurse anesthetists who take the weekend and holiday call. As a fellow, you will probably have night call only two or three times per month." He took approximately one hour to speak with me and gave me a tour of the operating rooms and intensive care unit. At the end of the tour, he said, "I have a good feeling about you. If you want it, the job is yours!"

I was not expecting that and was at a momentary loss for words. He spoke up and said, "I know that you need time to digest all of this, so here is my card. Call me in a few days, and let me know your decision."

I smiled, thanked him, and tried to stay grounded as I floated back into the locker room to change clothes. This had been a whirlwind two-and-a-half days of interviews, and I was catching an early flight Saturday morning.

Upon arrival at home, I noted that the mail had been delivered and the letterhead showed The Cardiac Center, Houston, Texas. My first thought was that I would have to decide which program to accept. Much to my chagrin the letter inside "thanked" me for my "interest" in the cardiac fellowship program at the Cardiac Center. Unfortunately, it went on to say that there were no positions available at that time.

I was only momentarily deflated because I had Rey's card in my purse and knew that I would be giving him a call first thing Monday morning accepting his offer! In July, Jarrett and I would be beginning our fellowships together in Texas but at different hospitals. Fortunately, we had saved a week of vacation to use at the end of our residencies in D.C. This allowed us to pack up, find a place, and drive to Houston to our new home.

I had been told about the heat and humidity of Houston and felt that it couldn't be any worse than what I had experienced in Washington, D.C. Wrong! Forty miles from downtown Houston, I felt as though I had just driven into a wet sauna whose calibrations were completely off, resulting in the feeling that the sun was sitting on the road, enveloping the car. Nevertheless, there was no turning back now.

For an adult, starting over in a new city is never easy, but going into a polar-opposite ethnic arena makes the transition even harder. I was no stranger to change. I had now experienced the world in a way I had never dreamed possible as a child. I had traveled to Washington, D.C., New York, Germany, France, Austria, and Switzerland in the years since graduating from high school. In spite of this, on these last few miles I allowed my mind to wander back into time when things were all the same.

There had been no worldly existence for me beyond the two-block radius that encompassed our house, my friends' houses, the church, and Mr. Perry's grocery store. With the exception of Mr. Perry, everyone in my world had looked just like me and my family, with the myriad skin tones ranging from coffee crème to dark chocolate mocha. Hair care also had similar requirements, of straightening combs to blast through the kinks, leaving me in tears because my kinks were tighter than those of anyone else I knew in the world. Home, that wooden three-room, shotgun structure, continued to be a comforting thought. I could see the kerosene lamps that everyone used for light, the potbellied coal-burning stove in the middle room for heat, the wood-burning stove in the kitchen for cooking, and the icebox used for keeping food cold. The ice man would come twice per week, and Momma would always purchase a twenty-five pound block for our icebox. We sometimes only bought ice once a week because we did not always have the ten cents necessary to pay for the ice. I never knew the economics of keeping the coal house full of coal for the winter, but there never seemed to be a time when we were without it. As a child, I had only glimpsed the other end of Hastings Street while walking to church. Buried deep inside my psyche, I knew that "decent" people would not be caught there due to the Bier Garten.

Regardless of the harshness of the reality of the economics of childhood, I still felt a sense of comfort in transporting my mind back to this simple time prior to my arrival in Houston. We had stopped in Memphis and hired a young lady to help with child care responsibilities. Our rented townhouse was across the street from an elementary school that Eriela could attend.

20 - WILLIE JOE

Little did I know that I was destined to cross paths with another Memphian, Willie Joe, who had also worked as the short-order cook at Cozy Inn many years after my momma had been there. In 1982, Cozy Inn had just served its last customer and the doors would be closed forever. Willie Joe's hopes of becoming a chef were finally extinguished. His position as short-order cook had never risen any higher, in spite of the Louisiana spices and sauces he had added to enhance the offerings of Cozy Inn's menu. Mr. Perry, the White owner, who had tried to bring some business back into Smokey City, had finally had enough of break-ins, robberies, and diminishing clientele. He thanked Willie Joe for his years of service, gave him one week's pay, and told him that he could have enough of the leftover food to eat for a couple of weeks.

Long hours in the hot kitchen, salt- and fat-filled diets, as well as genetics, had finally caught up with Willie Joe. Like many Black men, he found himself overweight, hypertensive, diabetic, and out of a job at the age of fifty. He knew that the one-week paycheck and the meager amount of money that he had managed to save would not last very long. Even though he had only finished sixth grade, his knowledge base of street survival far surpassed the average younger man on the street. He scoured newspapers, watched news on televisions sitting in store windows for sale, and listened in on conversations from other street people who had made their way across the country by hitchhiking or jumping on trains. It was from these sources that he found out about the oil boom and the huge medical center in Houston, Texas.

Willie Joe realized that his health condition would be a major contributor to the insurmountable odds he faced just to live if he couldn't get his diabetes and blood pressure medicines. "Where would these be in a goodly supply?" he wondered. It dawned on him that doctors and hospitals were the places he always had to go. If he was to have a continuing supply, he needed a job, with benefits. Cooking was the only thing he knew, and a doctor's office would surely have no need for a cook. A hospital, on the other hand, with patients and all the people who worked there, certainly needed to eat. The same was true for people on oil rigs. According to the information he had gathered, both of these businesses were in Houston. Surely an opportunity could present itself if he were there, and so he gathered his meager belongings and set off for Houston.

Upon arrival, there was no sight of oil rigs at which Willie Joe could inquire about a job, and the thought of going into those big company buildings like Enron downtown was just too daunting. He found his way to the Houston Medical Center with its huge complex of buildings, personnel, and supplies moving from place to place. In front of City Hospital, he saw all types of men loitering around the doors and felt that he wouldn't stick out like a sore thumb if he approached someone there.

As he gathered all his courage, he walked through the huge glass doors of The City hospital and went up to the first person he encountered, a white-coated man with a stethoscope around his neck.

"Scuse me suh, I needs to know where y'all do the hirin?"

As was not unusual for the South, the man looked through Willie Joe as though he were not there and walked on without giving a response. All the signs were a maze of colors, supposedly yielding directions to places within the hospital. Willie Joe found them very difficult to understand as he walked on.

A somewhat hefty, bent-over Black woman was pushing a cleaning cart as she approached Willie Joe.

"How do ma'am. I's lookin fuh de place they do the hirin," he said to her.

At close range she didn't look so old, and she definitely had some big jugs on her, with a butt that you could lay a tablecloth on.

Willie Joe thought to himself, "She might do more for me than direct me to the hirin office."

"I kin show ya," she said sweetly.

The sound of her husky southern drawl interrupted his musings.

"I sho thank ya, ma'am," he murmured as they ambled down the long corridor.

"What yo name?" he asked.

"Beulah," she replied, and continued: "I come up from Lusanna 'bout a year ago. The Lawd blessed me wid dis job den."

"I's a cook and figured they might gimme a job in da kitchen," Willie Joe said. She stopped and said, "You ain't heard? We ain't got no kitchen. Da flood messed up everythin' in the basement. Dey been havin companies brang in food fuh folks to eat."

Beulah remembered a conversation she had overheard at the bus stop and told Willie Joe: "Dey just fired a fellah who cleaned in the operating room over at The Private Hospital cuz he was sniffing stuff from the anesthesia machine. Miss Faye runs thangs up dere. Mebbe you can git his job."

Willie Joe couldn't believe his good fortune, and Beulah gave him more reason to beam as she said, smiling in her husky southern drawl, "I git off at 2:00 if you wanna know where a good roomin house is."

Willie Joe grinned broadly and said, "I jes might take you up on dat! Where you gon be when you git off?" Without saying a word, she nodded toward the bus stop and went on down the hall.

Willie Joe hustled, sweating and out of breath, to The Private Hospital and Miss Faye's office in the cardiothoracic operating room. As fate would have it, this was the first day of the rest of both of our lives, as he became the newest nursing assistant in the cardiothoracic operating room. I became the first African American Female Advanced Trainee in Cardiothoracic and Vascular Anesthesiology at The Private Hospital.

21 - FELLOWSHIP TRAINING – NEW WORLD ORDER

On the night before Jarrett and I started our fellowships, our household was filled with excitement and anticipation of our lives in Houston. Having stopped in Memphis and hired a young lady to come with us and take care of our children, we were busy with instructions for the children's days as we began our advanced training. Though it was a hot summer in Houston, the neighborhood playground was across the street. It was only a short walk to the zoo, so we felt there would be ample opportunities for them to get out of the house and do some fun things while we were at work. Eriela was a bookworm and would have been content to sit in the bay window and read all day, but Jai needed to run and exercise her imagination as she searched for imaginary bears.

Therefore it was important that they both be taken outside of the house and be exposed to the wonders of nature. Emergency contact numbers were posted on the refrigerator. That first night, the girls had their baths and were put to bed.

Jarret and I lay there talking and lamenting the fact that we would be in separate hospitals for the first time in our relationship. Gone would be the surprise meetings in the elevators yielding a quick kiss, lunching together in the cafeteria, and cuddly time in the call room if one of us was on call. In addition to the little personal touches we had experienced at work, we knew that the institutional change would be magnanimous! We were leaving a 100 percent African American professional workplace and entering a 99.9 percent White American professional workplace.

Sleep was slow to come for me that night, and when it did, I felt quite restless. Jarrett, on the other hand, went off to sleep within two minutes of the end of our last conversation.

The morning arrived and I dressed quickly for work, kissed my sleeping angels, and went out the door to start my advanced training in cardiothoracic anesthesiology.

Fellowship life was officially about to start for me, and signing papers as well as attending College of Medicine orientation had taken up the first part of the morning. I then ran the two blocks to The Private Hospital and arrived breathlessly for my first day in the cardiothoracic unit.

The automatic double doors swung open to the operating suite. The front desk, manned by a clerk and a charge nurse, was immediately to the right as I walked in. Standing next to the assignment board directly in front of me, in his muted green scrubs, was Dr. Rey. He smiled and said, "Good morning Ruth! I was beginning to wonder if you had changed your mind!"

"No sir! I ..." was all I could get out before he said, "I know about College of Medicine orientations. They have historically taken a very long time." I breathed an audible sigh of relief. He continued, "I hope you signed up to take the maximum out of your check for your retirement plan. As I mentioned in our phone conversation, you don't want to give up free money from the College of Medicine."

I had read that for an employee's maximum salary deduction of 5 percent, the hospital would match with a maximum of 7 percent of salary, from college funds. After ignoring the Xerox advice from the manager of my summer job, I was not going to make the same mistake twice!

I responded, "Absolutely, I don't want to refuse free money!" He then told me that we could talk more later, but right now I should get dressed for the OR and report to room 7, where a big case had already started and could use an extra pair of hands. As I looked back on that day, it was interesting to note that I was already being viewed as a body part – a pair of hands! Any medical knowledge that I may have had was already discounted.

I went into the women's locker room, took a pair of blue scrubs off of the cart, and dressed for my maiden voyage into the operating theater. All of the anesthesiology personnel, with the exception of

Dr. Rey, wore blue scrubs.

This first case that I was assigned to as an "extra pair of hands" was a repair of a thoracoabdominal aortic aneurysm. It was well underway when I walked into operating room 7. Lying on the operating table was a patient who had been cut from underneath his arm and around to his abdomen down to his belly button. My eyes were wide as two saucers! I could see everything in the chest cavity and quite a bit of the abdominal cavity! Intravenous lines were hanging everywhere! I saw two at the feet, one on each arm, and one in the neck! The surgeon had just clamped and opened the aorta. Blood was everywhere! The anesthesiologist and nurse anesthetist were busy giving drugs and hanging blood and other fluids.

The surgeon would periodically ask, "How's he doing?"

The anesthesiologist would reply, "Stable."

I was then given a multitude of orders.

"Draw a blood gas."

"Take some plasma and hang it on the foot IV."

"Hang some bicarb."

"Check the blood gas result."

"Keep up with the chart."

I had never seen this type of surgery, and had had only a brief tour of this operating room (which was unlike any I had ever seen before); I was totally overwhelmed!

Meanwhile, there was minimal oral communication between the surgeon (who I later learned was the famous Saul Levinsky) and his scrub nurse. She seemed to know and have ready each instrument or suture he would need next. Occasionally, she would place a suction catheter into the hand of one of his assistants and point to the area where blood was beginning to well up. This dance of surgeon and nurse was executed as though they had perfected it as a well-choreographed production on Broadway. When most of the preparatory work had been done inside the patient, the scrub nurse would hand the surgeon a couple of Dacron grafts (a tubular material that would not allow any type of fluid to pass through its sides). He would select the appropriate one to reconnect the sections of this patient's aorta. After a brief moment of inspection and checking of size, the surgeon would inform the scrub nurse of the specific graft he would need. The circulating nurse would retrieve a sterile copy and hand it off to the sterile table of the scrub nurse. The surgeon would give a final inspection, pour albumin solution over it, and hand it back to the scrub nurse. She sent it out of the room with the circulating nurse to be "cooked" in the autoclave. An autoclave is a heater-like machine that brings items placed inside it to an extremely high temperature and pressure for the purpose of sterilization. When the cooked graft was returned, the surgeon's hands really took flight! Sutures were placed around the circumference of the graft so rapidly and with such precision that one would have thought that a sewing machine had done the deed. I later came to realize that this speed was necessary once the aorta was clamped because all blood supply to the lower body had been cut off (ischemia). Prolonged periods of ischemia could result in kidney failure and paralysis of the legs and feet.

This critical period allowed all personnel in the operating room to fill their dance cards with their own versions of immediacy and expectancy. The anesthesiologist's brain went into overdrive as pharmaco-physiologic planning was actuated. The heart needed to be overly filled with blood and fluids to accommodate the vacuum left by the empty blood vessels that had been standing idly by. This lack of movement through the system also led to large increases of acid build-up in the lower part of the body. Such a huge acid load, if left untreated, could result in catastrophic changes to the body's internal chemistries, leading to dangerously low blood pressure or death.

The circulating nurses were in constant motion as they anticipated the need for additional sutures, cloth sponges, and instruments in the sterile field. Periodically, their voices could be heard over the intercom announcing "nursing assistant to room 7." After having been given the requests, the nursing assistants could be seen rapidly approaching the room with blood or blood products, and leaving with vials of blood destined for the lab. The lab information allowed up-to-the-minute tweaking of the pharmacological plan by the anesthesia team. Very little talking was going on because those in the room knew their roles.

The pronouncement by the surgeon of "head down" heralded the completion of the graft connection. A key piece of anesthetic management for this phase was to place the operating table in a position such that the head of the bed would be lowered down toward the floor, while the feet were aimed at the ceiling. The graft was pricked with small needle-holes, allowing tiny blood spurts to leap into the air prior to beginning their circuitous journey through the body. All of these preparations were necessary to ensure that all air bubbles were out of the blood vessels, and the brain and heart could be protected from catastrophic air effects. With clamp removal, the blood pressure would always drop precipitously, as though it had just fallen off a mountainside. However, prior volume loading and correction of the acid build-up in the body shortened this extremely low blood pressure period. Finely tuned pharmacologic and physiologic management allowed the anesthesiologist to once again restore the patient to "stable vital signs," with minimal bleeding.

Dr. Levinsky left the remainder of this case to his assistants to finish up. The surgical team completed the closure by sewing up all the layers of the patient's incision, placed dressings, and aided in transporting the patient to the intensive care unit.

This first fellowship training experience took me into a realm of anesthesiology and surgery that I never really knew existed. Nothing comparable to the magnitude of this procedure occurred during my medical education and residency

Cleaning the cardiothoracic operating room required many hands. AIDS had not become the known deadly entity in that day. Personnel would be splattered with blood on scrubs, masks, faces, hats, and hands. Machinery, walls, floors, and sometimes even the ceiling had to be cleansed of pools of blood that appeared to have been made on purpose, in geometric designs. As one of the nursing assistants cleaning on this day, Willie Joe began wielding the huge mop to clean the floor. He was in such a rush to show how well and quickly he worked that he missed a pool of blood underneath the operating table. Henrietta, the RN who was also the scrub nurse, realized it was there just as she was repositioning the bed for the next case.

A loud scream erupted with the words, "Are you retarded?"

We all turned and saw that it was coming from Henrietta. Her face was twisted in such a mask of rage that she was almost unrecognizable!

"You have to be the dumbest nursing assistant ever hired here! Who do you think is going to come behind you to do your work?" she continued loudly. "Would you want to come in and lay on top of someone else's blood while you were being operated on? Get your lazy tail out of here!"

Another nursing assistant quickly moved over to clean up the remaining blood and move the bed to ensure that no more blood was there. He then moved the bed back near its proper place.

I was mortified that a professional African American woman could belittle an African American man so publicly and in such a despicable way. Hoping to deflect some of the venomous attack, I quickly moved the mop bucket toward the door as I nudged Willie Joe toward the doorway. He seemed paralyzed by the suddenness of the malice being directed at him. I quietly walked over to her and introduced myself. When she turned to face me, I asked Henrietta if I could help. This singular moment caused Henrietta's barrage of insults to stop. Willie Joe was able to finish the room turnover by bringing in new plastic hampers without additional comment. He silently thanked God for this angel who had come to his rescue and vowed to repay her in some way. It appeared as if the forewarnings that I had heard about the surgeons could be applied to the nursing personnel as well!

What an auspicious beginning for me! Though not as bloody, my next case, a coronary artery bypass, was equally tense. Dr. Levinsky was again the faculty operating surgeon. His assistants performed all the preliminary procedures: opening the chest, harvesting the veins for bypass, and preparing the patient for the heart-lung machine. My faculty member had already administered the heparin, which would keep the blood from clotting. Dr. Levinsky came in and was gowned and gloved by the scrub nurse. After inquiring as to the readiness of the patient for bypass and receiving an affirmative answer from my faculty member, he released all clamps, initiating cardiopulmonary bypass. The heart-lung machine had officially taken over the job of the human heart and lungs. My only function for this case was to chart the patient's vital signs. It was getting close to 3:00 p.m. when Dr. Rey walked in and told me that I could leave for the day. By this time, all my nerves were tense and coiled. I felt that I was tight enough to have passed for a violin and been played! On the drive home, my brain couldn't process all that I had been involved in at work because of the complexity of the operations and the behavior of the battle-weary personnel.

Once I reached home, I could not dwell on the events of the day because now I needed to change hats and become only housewife and mommy. We were fortunate that it was summertime, and we did not yet have to deal with school issues. As I was preparing dinner, I was inquiring about the girls' day. In spite of all the plans that had been laid out for them, they still spent the entire day inside. The language of a soon-to-be two-year-old was not yet clear, and her breakfast request of "kee heet" could not be deciphered by the babysitter. She had emptied the entire content of the pantry shelves trying to locate it with a screaming child in front of her, who also had lost patience for the adult who would not give her breakfast! Eriela finally tired of the screaming and kitchen noises, and went downstairs to inform the sitter that Jai wanted "Cream of Wheat"! The morning was totally used up by the time she had everything back in the cabinets and in order.

By the afternoon, the temperature had risen to 105 degrees, allowing sitter and kids only a two-block walk before they turned around to get back inside to air conditioning. All our planning was for naught, and this did not sit well with me! I decided that I needed to give all our situations some adjustment time.

As I trained to become a cardiothoracic anesthesiologist and juggled the roles of mommy and wife, my every waking moment was full. It soon became obvious that this babysitter was not going to work out. The Bourbon family, whom Jarrett had met in high school, was instrumental in helping to find a replacement for her. They introduced us to Auntie M., who was a life-saver in the first few months of adjustment to our lives in Houston. Since the school was across the street from our townhouse, Eriela could walk to school each day during the first few months while we were waiting for the purchase of our home to go through. When the sale was finalized and the move made to our new home across town, we hired a Swedish woman who had a one-year-old child to drive Eriela to school and do the housework. Mila, the Swedish woman, initially was grateful to have a place to live and eat and drink. She and her daughter alone consumed three gallons of milk a week! Though they were given a small guest house out back, they were constantly coming inside the main house and encroaching on the privacy of our nuclear family when we were at home. Because of the long hours, extremely ill patients, and very stressful working conditions and the necessity for help, we decided to ignore these things for a while.

I became more comfortable with the operating suite and the nursing personnel. Periodically, pharmaceutical representatives brought lunch in for everyone, and some of the nurses always invited me into their lounge to get some of the lunch. With the exception of the surgeons, the ethnicity of the operating room personnel was multinational. The Philippines, Thailand, South America, and of course the United States, were all represented. I used the same dressing room as the nurses, and we often had conversations about our families and interests outside of the job. This gave me some modicum of comfort that someone would talk with me without putting me down! Initially, the anesthesiology personnel were not quite as welcoming. I felt that I was in a fishbowl, with everyone watching my every move and waiting for me to do something wrong.

The stresses and strains of trying to "fit in" at work while being a good wife and mother were tremendous. I had to fight the urge to quit my job every day of my first two months.

During my third month on the job, another fellow-in-training, from France, was hired. We clicked immediately. He became my support person at work and encouraged me to continue with the fellowship each time that I wanted to quit. Around this same time, I learned that I had not achieved a passing rate on my written board examinations, which I had taken at the end of my first week on the job.

Because I had not passed the anesthesiology written-portion leading to board certification, I was weighed down with the emotional drain of feelings of inadequacy. The time came to begin preparations to take my boards again, and due to my haphazardly long and busy work schedule, I had to use the weekends to read, take practice exams, and study with a friend who was also preparing to take the exam. When spring arrived, we decided to study at a location away from our homes, without the distractions of family. Mila decided to press her need for the use of my car since it was the weekend and her "off days."

After I told her that would not be possible over the next few months due to my study schedule, she looked at me with a face twisted by indignity and said, "I will have to pack my bags!"

I could not believe that yet another human, especially one that I was paying, was trying to put her needs ahead of my own! I turned and looked at her with a cold, steely glare and said, "Okay."

She continued even more loudly, "I mean that I will have to leave."

I could imagine my head turning on its axis just as the actress had in The Exorcist. I then responded more forcefully, "Okay, how much time do you need, one week or two?!" She was visibly shaken and flabbergasted that someone who needed her assistance as much as I did could respond so negatively and so quickly. She stammered, "One week." I calmly turned, picked up my books, got into my car, and sped down the driveway as if I were on the INDY 500 raceway!

Upon my return, she came to me saying, "We have to talk."

I said, "I am all talked out, and I want you out by the end of the week, at the latest!" Unfortunately for her, she didn't realize that my daily grind in the operating room had quickly zapped all of my energy. My self-confidence was at an all-time low! I could not afford to have outside negativism under my own roof destroy my much-needed oasis at home. When I arrived home each day after leaving the hellhole in which I worked, my home became a satisfying, refreshing, cool pool like those found in the middle of the Sahara. Spring break occurred the following week and gave me an opportunity to find someone else to take my daughter to school when it resumed.

The battle to find a good balance between work and personal life continued.

Each day that I drove to work was akin to driving knowingly to one of the trains bound for Auschwitz. The true characters of the anesthesiology and surgical staff were beginning to show. As I arrived at work each day, I didn't know in which direction my armor should be focused! I was rotated around to work with each of the various anesthesiology faculty. It was not until much later that I realized that I was not being rotated through all of the surgeons.

22 - LEARNING THE ROPES WHILE NAVIGATING MINEFIELDS

When I arrived in the operating room this particular day, I saw that I had been assigned to work with Dr. Zepeda as my faculty. Dr. Zepeda was a temperamental, egomaniacal South American anesthesiologist whose emotions spiraled out of control on a daily basis. I had heard that one evening he became so angry with one of the surgeons that he grabbed four bags of the heart-protecting cardioplegia and threw them into the room at the surgeon's feet! After displaying this pitching prowess, he turned around, pulled his pants down, and mooned the surgeon with his bare bottom!

I recognized the ludicrous behavior that he was capable of exhibiting, and knew exactly where my protective armor should be focused. As with most of the cases in this operating room, managing a patient for a valve replacement required extensive monitoring of the patient's heart functions. Advanced trainees, such as I, were normally allowed to put in place pulmonary artery catheters (advance monitors of heart function), under the supervision of the faculty in charge of the case. The patient that Dr. Zepeda and I were responsible for also required this monitor for his impending heart valve replacement surgery. The preoperative work-up revealed that this patient had been experiencing heartbeats originating in many different abnormal sites in his heart, with occasional runs of fast pumping of the left ventricle, a seriously severe heart rhythm problem. It was difficult for Dr. Zepeda to allow any trainee to perform procedures, especially me, and he constantly criticized every move that I made, from the beginning of the case.

"Why are you using a Macintosh blade for intubation? Don't you know that anyone who knows anything about anesthesiology uses a straight blade?" Zepeda said rather loudly, trying to belittle me in front of the entire room.

I bristled slightly and clenched my jaws, but said nothing and proceeded to intubate the patient (place a tube in his throat for breathing) and secure the breathing tube with tape.

"Don't tape the tube like that!" he screamed. "You're going to get me sued for damaging the patient's teeth!"

My heart began to pound rapidly and forcefully from this assault on the most elementary of skills. Emotionally, I was slipping deeper and deeper into a black abyss from which it would be difficult to return. I forced myself to hold my tongue. I stepped back without uttering a word and allowed him to remove the tape and position the endotracheal tube as he desired. He began swabbing the neck with Betadine while I stood there.

He turned to me and barked, "Don't stand there like a dummy. Get your gown and gloves on!"

I could feel sweat coating my chest and underarms. Again, I held my tongue. Was my action the model of peaceful acceptance in the face of bodily assaults, espoused by Dr. Martin Luther King during the civil rights movement? Was this a lesson that I could have learned had I been among the battle-weary young Black people who participated in sit-ins and crossed picket lines during the 1960s, only to be attacked by dogs and fire hoses? I gowned up and readied the table for placement of the pulmonary artery catheter. I isolated the internal jugular vein and proceeded to place the guide wire. The patient began to have bursts of irregular heart rhythms.

When Zepeda noted this on the monitor, he began screaming, "Take it out! Take it out!"

I responded by removing the wire and the sheath.

Zepeda became beet-red and shouted, "Why did you do that?"

I calmly stated, "You said take it out."

Zepeda then screamed, "I didn't mean everything. Now what are we going to do?"

My attempt at peaceful acceptance went the way of the dodo bird as I looked directly into his eyes and with an icy cold voice said, "I don't know. You're the staff. You put it in."

With that said, I tore off my gown and gloves and walked out of the room. Though my actions were quiet and deliberate, I am certain that the rage I incited in Dr. Zepeda was anything but quiet!

The loudspeakers in the hallway erupted, "Anesthesia, room 3!" "Dr. Rey, room 3!"

Dr. Rey and one of the nurse anesthetists ran past me, barreling down the hall toward room 3 as I proceeded on calmly to the lounge. The speaker from the room was still on, and to the casual observer who was listening in, World War III had just erupted in room 3.

Dr. Zepeda was screaming, among other things, "Either she has to go, or I will go!" Dr. Rey had to use his most diplomatic persona to soothe this situation over. He switched my assignment for the remainder of that day and replaced me with the nurse anesthetist who had accompanied him to the room.

I was able to complete the remainder of that day without any further histrionics from other faculty.

Since I recognized Dr. Zepeda's flair for the dramatic, I was successful in not internalizing this most recent assault on my abilities. I also learned to be more proactive in my preparatory work, so as to minimize the need for faculty input with minor setup procedures.

☐

Dr. Willingham

Though there were periods of calm at work, someone always stepped up to ensure that I knew I didn't belong there.

The operating room suite was populated primarily by White male surgeons and could be termed, "A Bastion of Male Superiority." One of the female anesthesiologists, Dr. Willingham, had the same superiority complex and was just as demanding as Zepeda. Though she didn't carry on the histrionics that he did, she always mandated how she wanted things to go during various procedures. She, too, was a big proponent of the use of a straight blade for intubation, crisscross taping of intravenous and atrial catheters, as well as head position for intubation. Her interventions were primarily silent protestations, delivered with body language while removing and re-taping, as though I was a child, or slapping my hand so that she could place a shoulder roll. All equipment for insertion, whether peripherally or centrally, was prepared by her so that there would be no misunderstanding on what was to be used! I was on a steep learning curve and quickly learned her particular nuances in patient management.

With the exception of the chief, Dr. Willingham was the most senior anesthesiologist on the service. She was the "go to" person for all the surgeons, whether it was a complicated case or a rich head of state from another country. Though married to an American, she felt entitled to special treatment because of her distant -- very distant -- relationship to the Saudi royal family. Her golden bangles, jeweled earrings, and necklaces were, in her mind, visible proof of such an alignment! Though she smiled to my face, I knew that she was a disingenuous type.

I had finished setting up my room and was taking the back hall to return to the pre-op area to see my patient. Willie Joe was coming down the back hall after having finished cleaning a room.

"Can I talk to you fuh a minute?"

"Sure", I said. "But only a minute because I have to finish seeing my patient."

He continued, saying, "While I was mopping room one, I heard Dr. Willen talking to dat fat anesthesia nurse bout you. Watch yo back. They don't mean you no good."

"Thanks Willie Joe, I will certainly do that!" My blood pressure rose a few notches as I walked on down the hallway. Neither Dr. Willingham nor the nurse anesthetist could see my approach. Upon hearing my name, I stopped long enough to hear this part of the conversation.

"Can you believe they hired her?" stated Willingham.

"Whenever I am assigned with her, I make sure that all of my lines are in before she arrives. I don't want anyone blaming me for her multiple pokes in a patient's arm," said the nurse anesthetist.

After that statement, I quickly rounded the corner so that they could see me. My face showed pure fury. I addressed the nurse first. "If you had the smarts to receive an MD, you would not have to be supervised. The skill set that you are quick to point out as your supposed expertise can be taught to a monkey. Given the amount of time that you have been working here, you must be pretty slow since you have no other expertise to brag about." To both I said, "If I ever hear either of you maligning my abilities or my character again, you will be slapped with a lawsuit so fast that it will make your head spin!"

I did a quick about face so that they could not see the tears welling up in my eyes. The vow from my youth resurfaced: no matter what came my way, no one would ever see me cry! With tears so close to falling, I knew that I had to hasten my efforts to develop a thick skin. Obviously mine needed to rival that of elephant hide!

During this year of training, I developed the ability to remain calm and not to be as combative as I had been with Dr. Zepeda nor as confrontational as I had been with Dr. Willingham. I came to realize that there were many ways to do everything required of me in the operating room. There were those who demanded that a shoulder roll be placed prior to the insertion of a catheter into the subclavian vein. Others thought that shoulder rolls were entirely unnecessary and not very practical. Some required a splint prior to placing an arterial catheter. Others said a splint caused too much extension and took the artery out of its natural plane. Some used catheters over needles to locate the internal jugular vein. Others preferred to use a steel needle.

There were seven anesthesiology faculty members, various types of needles, catheters, tapes, and drapes in the cardiothoracic operating room. Each faculty member had his or her own rationale for which was better to use. During my fellowship training year, I learned all seven of their techniques and preferences and which one to use when I worked with each of them. My mantra was "equanimity under duress." After all, my plan was that this would only last one year and I would seek employment elsewhere after this training period was over.

As the end of the fall approached and the time for end-of-year job search arrived, my first request was to join the obstetric anesthesiology section of the department. The chairman told me that he would let me know after he had his budget approved. In the early spring, I saw an advertisement by the University Teaching Hospital seeking anesthesiologists. I was excited that this could be a possibility for me. I mailed in my application and was granted an interview. When I walked into the office of the doctor in charge of faculty recruitment, an immediate chill permeated the air.

He gave me a cursory look up and down and stated, "Unfortunately, you are overqualified for what we need. Thank you for your interest."

With that said, he stood up and walked out of the room. I was flabbergasted. Never in my wildest dreams had I thought that someone could be "overqualified" as an anesthesiologist, especially in a university setting! Oh well, I must return to the "dungeon" of my old cardiothoracic unit and begin my quest anew to secure a position.

During the early part of April, my chairman called me in and stated, "We still have not received funding for our OB unit. However, a position will be available at The Private Hospital's Cardiac Unit, where you have been training. You are now familiar with their routines, and I can offer you a position over there when you finish in June." I stared at him incredulously thinking, "Is he crazy? Who in their right mind would want to work in that cesspool of a place?"

The silence was deafening. To bridge the silence, he said, "I know this is not your first choice, but why not try it? You've worked here for a year and are familiar with the place and its routines. If you don't like it, we can transfer you later."

Remembering my experience with the other university teaching hospital, I realized that this was the only game in town at the moment. With total resignation, I quietly replied, "Thank you, I'll take the position."

Dr. Rey took the month of June off. By that time, it was known that I had been hired to join the staff in July. During Dr. Rey's absence, Dr. Nance, another anesthesiology faculty, sauntered up to me and said, "Ruth, you should rethink your decision to work here. These surgeons are a difficult bunch to work with. You will most certainly have so many battles to fight that I won't be able to help you with them."

The level of confidence that I had taken so long to reach was destroyed as completely as a glass falling on stone. Though the precise words were not spoken, it was crystal clear that my presence on the faculty was not wanted in this operating room. I quickly reconciled myself to the disingenuous nature of my colleague, who was always smiling in my face as though I had been accepted as one of the team. This verbal interchange and his body language showed his true feelings as they came galloping to the forefront! While this latest emotional assault was reverberating in my brain, I knew that it could not be left unanswered.

Again, the steel in my back hardened and I replied, "I haven't asked you to fight any battle for me. I can fight my own battles with these surgeons. And if necessary, I'll fight you too!"

Little did I know that a new sheriff was coming to town! By the end of June, Dr. Rey had been replaced as Chief of the Cardiothoracic Service by Dr. Nance. My previous conversation with Dr. Nance would reverberate in my head for a very long time and cause even more insecurity about the longevity (or lack thereof) for my employment!

One of the other, more welcoming, faculty heard the exchange and later came up to me and said, "Ruth, I want you to know that because you are Black and a woman, you had to be twice as good as the average applicant before you could be offered a faculty position here! In time, things will get better for you."

§ § §

"No one can make you feel inferior without your permission," Eleanor Roosevelt

23 - MEMBER OF THE FACULTY

I started my faculty assignment in July, and I was also scheduled to take my written anesthesiology boards in July. As had occurred during my first year there, I was scheduled to be on resident emergency call the night before the exam. The rationale given for this assignment was that faculty had to cover the operating rooms for the residents who would be taking their "in-training exams" at the same time. The in-training exam scores were a reflection of the residency training program, and every effort had to be made to ensure that residents could do their best. The other faculty, who had been there a minimum of ten years, was already board certified, and according to Dr. Nance, no allowances had been made for them. I was told that I needed to plan better when I needed time off. I should, then, request vacation days for important matters such as this well in advance! My previous conversation with Dr. Nance should have provided a forewarning on the lack of consideration that I would receive. It still stung to be hit in the face with it so quickly. I knew that I had to put on my big-girl panties and be prepared for whatever came my way!

Catapulting the great divide from trainee to trainer was not a simple task, at least intellectually! As I drove to work that first morning, the tension that I'd felt as a fellow was a walk in the park compared to the knots in my stomach and neck that I was now experiencing as a first-time faculty. When I arrived, I noted to my relief that I had been assigned only one case to staff with a resident. At that point, coronary artery bypass cases were relatively easy to manage, and having done so many virtually alone during my fellowship year, I had become comfortable with them. As the case progressed, I, along with my resident, got into the rhythm of the work, and my inner coils began to release a bit of their tension. Unfortunately for the resident, this was more of a demonstration day than an actual hands-on day for him. Other than insertion of the peripheral intravenous catheter and the endotracheal intubation, I performed all the other technical procedures: intra-arterial, subclavian, and internal jugular vein catheterizations. Oh my, had I become a carbon copy of the faculty that I had trained under?! I remained in the room the entire case, while allowing coffee breaks for my resident. By 1:00 p.m., my bladder was crying uncle! To me and my bladder's relief, the case went smoothly, and we were able to settle the patient safely in the ICU, at which time I raced to the toilet! Since I had been exposed to primarily twelve-hour days as a fellow, I was mentally prepared for the long hours, which on occasion stretched longer than that.

Over the previous year, I had also had at least minimal exposure to all of the surgeons. Now that I was a full-fledged faculty member, the "hand holding," such as it was, would no longer occur. I had to sink or swim with sharks.

24 - PROFESSIONAL RELATIONSHIPS WITH SENIOR SURGEONS

I soon learned that though I had the title of faculty, with its inferred professionalism, my day-to-day work life was far from that of an equal professional! I categorized our relationships into three major categories: Continuously Malignant, Callously Indifferent, and Appreciatively Accepting. As the younger surgical fellows finished their training, with a very few being accepted to work in this grand world of power, our relationships also had minor twists of negative challenges.

Only two of the senior surgeons could be categorized as continuously malignant, Dr. Moritz Gregorian and Dr. Joe Lee Hayward.

As time passed, I heard that I had not been the only trainee who was burdened by unreasonable and difficult faculty. My fellow surgical trainees had had their fair share of trauma at the hands of their faculty, too.

Senior Surgeons Exhibiting Continuous Malignancy

Dr. Moritz Gregorian

Dr. Moritz Gregorian should have been labeled a borderline sociopath. On this day, the rumor mill was rampant with his antics. He became extremely angry with the inadequate exposure that his resident provided. Suddenly, he leaned across the table, butting the poor resident in the head with his head! Bone could be heard crashing into bone with each head butt! Dr. Rey came into the room and said, "Moritz, I hear we have to provide football helmets for your residents!" By then, all of the air had been sucked out of the room. No one dared utter a sound. Emboldened by the presence of my most senior anesthesiology faculty, I did at least put a Cheshire cat grin on my face! Dr. Gregorian responded to Dr. Rey, "These dumb son-of-a-bitches need to learn how to operate." With that small interchange having ended, Dr. Rey left the room and the case proceeded on as though nothing out of the ordinary had happened! On a later date, Dr. Gregorian became so worked up over the inadequacy of surgical exposure that he snatched the surgical instrument out of the resident's hand and proceeded to beat that hand with it. The poor resident continued to work for the rest of the day, and only after work did he go to have it checked out. The hand was found to be broken! It was only after this incident that the "powers that be" stepped in and removed all trainees from his service.

I wondered why he was never sued. After some surreptitious investigation, I found that residents were afraid to sue. They feared that they would not be able to finish their training programs nor get a job after training if any of these shenanigans were brought to light!

As luck would have it, my baptism by fire as a faculty from the surgical side was initiated by Dr. Moritz Gregorian. By way of additional introduction, it should be noted that Dr. Gregorian was such an egomaniac that he preached on many occasions that the only perfect surgery that could occur would happen only if he cloned himself to become the nursing staff, perfusion staff, and anesthesiology staff!

Under normal circumstances, the nursing staff was always tasked with setting up the surgical table and arranging the instruments and towels which were to be used during the surgery. The scrub nurse would always hand the instruments to the surgeon during the operative procedure. Dr. Gregorian, on the other hand, would take a group of instruments and place them on a magnetic mat on top of the patient, rather than accepting them from the scrub nurse. Whenever he became angry, he would throw instruments onto the floor, necessitating re-sterilization by the nursing staff. One of his favorite sayings after having depleted the operative field of instruments was, "When you are down to four, get more! Send somebody to the City Teaching Saint!" He was referring to the University Teaching hospital, the competition for our hospital, which was several blocks down the street.

My first case with him involved the use of fluoroscopy, and he mandated that I turn off the ventilator and leave the room. My resident was out on a break. I thought he was crazy! I had never left a paralyzed patient alone in a room before! Initially I refused to leave. He screamed again, "Dammit, didn't I tell you to cut off the ventilator?"

Reluctantly and with mixed emotions, I turned off the ventilator and stepped outside of the windowed door for the minute that it took for the fluoroscopy to occur. When I returned, he mumbled, "Where are we getting them from now – Bangladesh?" Inside, I wanted to explode and fire back some equally derogatory comment, but adult reasoning intervened, making me hold my tongue. Though we never actually never spiraled out of control into shouting matches, we each felt the intense dislike that emanated from the other whenever we worked together. I heard that he had labeled me as passive-aggressive, but he never spoke directly to me again in all the years that I subsequently worked there. For my part, I used the minimalist approach in communicating with him, too!

Because of his previous shenanigans, he was forced to hire additional help. The second associate that he hired, who had not trained in our operating room, was as much an egomaniac as he was. On this particular day, Dr. Gregorian had finished the bypass grafts on the heart and left the new junior associate to close and finish up, while he went to another room to start another case with his other associate. Before leaving, he told the associate to make sure that he took the lap from behind the heart. The lap is a cloth used to soak up fluid and blood from the operative field. It was always the policy that the nurses would repeat the count of instruments, needles, and laps at the end of the case to ensure that everything was accounted for. The count was off, and they told this to the junior associate. He said, "There is nothing in the chest cavity," as he proceeded to close the patient's chest. The nurse informed him that an X-ray would have to be taken prior to taking the patient out of the room. He became agitated and restated that there was nothing left in the chest cavity. He continued to close the chest, with an air about him that indelibly depicted nurses as ignorant. He still had to wait for the X-ray. After it was done, it clearly showed that the lap Dr. Gregorian had mentioned was still behind the heart.

I said, "Dr. Gregorian told you to take that lap out before you closed."

He angrily turned to me and said, "You had better shut the fuck up before I have you wearing this lap."

Whoa! With that statement, my insides flushed as hot as fire! My heart felt as though it was going to jump out of my chest! My nostrils flared like those of a raging bull, and all of my quiet, lady-like reserve left me! Every ounce of my Smokey City ghetto upbringing rose up and spewed forth. The only person who appeared to recognize the line that had been crossed was my nurse anesthetist. I began leaning across the table as I said, "I might be wearing that lap, but I will mop this operating room up with your ass!" My verbal assault shocked him into silence, along with the remainder of the personnel in the room. My nurse anesthetist started pulling my top and pleading, "Don't hit him! Please don't hit him, Dr. Ruth!"

"Mr. junior associate surgeon" appeared to shrink toward the floor as all of his original bluster quickly dissipated! He quickly reclosed the patient's chest and left without saying another word to me. I'm sure that his ego was sorely bruised after being threatened by a mere woman who was half his size.

For a week, I heard from various surgeons in the operating room, "Dr. Ruth, I hear that you were going to kick some ass the other day!" I would revert to my quiet lady-like state and say, "It was just a small misunderstanding. Everything is fine."

My response to this situation showed that I was learning to take care of myself, no matter which bully presented himself! Though I had experienced a frontal emotional assault, I felt that I had come out on top. There was a lightness to my step as I went home to my family.

Dr. Joe Lee Hayward

Emergency night-call had been seemingly everlasting the previous night! Even though the cases were not particularly demanding, the surgeons operating were particularly slow to stop the bleeding on cases that had to be brought back to the operating room. I finally left at 5:00 a.m. Arriving home forty-five minutes before my family was to awaken to start their day was no fun, either. I tiptoed into the house and threw myself face down on the couch to get a few winks before anyone woke up. As soon as I heard the rustle of awakenings, I put my game face on and went in to sing the good-morning song to my younger daughter. I knew that the older one, the teenager, would have to be pulled out of bed with a crowbar! After the preliminary morning rituals with my children, my housekeeper bustled them out the door and on the way to school. My husband gave me a quick kiss as he too bounded out the door to go to work. I took this opportunity to close all the shutters, unplug the phone, and snuggle in very deeply under the covers of my bed.

Later that evening, as we were all lounging around the house prior to preparing for bed, the telephone rang.

"Dr. Ruth, this is Maurice, the pharmacist. A patient of Dr. Hayward has crashed in the cath lab, and the nurse anesthetist can't reach the faculty on call. Can you come in to help?" came the hurried voice over the phone.

"Of course," I responded and quickly jumped into a pair of jeans and a sweatshirt. "All hell is breaking loose at the hospital, and I am going in to help," I yelled as I was going out the door. I saw the look of dismay on my husband's face but did not wait to hear the words that were about to come from his open mouth. He, as well as I, was well aware of my previous long night on duty in the hospital.

Joe Lee Hayward, MD, was the supreme racist and sexist of all the surgeons on our unit. In referring to me, he had been quoted as saying that "Having her around is like having a black cat walk into the room!" He seemed to feel that all the nurses in the operating room and ICU were his personal playground for feeling them up! Walking up to one of them and giving their butt a squeeze was as normal as anyone else saying good morning. They never seemed to complain, and most even giggled with some degree of joy! I guess they felt this was supposed to happen in a bastion of male superiority. In addition to this, he treated the sterile operating room as though it were his home den. To check on the progress of the underlings who started cases for him, he would sometimes walk into the room wearing his outside lab coat. If that wasn't bad enough, his nicotine habit would cause him to hold his lit cigarette behind his back while peering into the operative field! We were lucky that no fires were ever started due to this carelessness in the presence of oxygen!

As I arrived in the operating room that night, the patient from the cardiac catheterization lab was being wheeled into the room. He had been placed on a portable cardiopulmonary bypass pump while in the cath lab. I took over the position at the head of the table from the nurse anesthetist and helped to get him settled onto the operating table.

The operating room nurses were still opening sterile equipment packs of instruments needed for the emergency open-heart bypass procedure. One of them ran over to pour Betadine on the patient's chest while the surgical team ran out to wash their hands. There was no time for a proper scrub of either the patient's chest or their hands.

A second pump technician was quickly assembling the larger cardiopulmonary bypass pump, which had been standing in its usual spot at the right side of operating bed, ready to be called into action as needed. When the patient did not have the capacity to circulate blood or oxygen on his own, this pump could perform that lifesaving function. On a normal day, two or three pump technicians would have it ready, by attaching its sterile containers, fluid, and tubing within a matter of a few minutes. Unfortunately, this was not daytime, when we would have had a plethora of personnel available.

The other technician was managing the settings of the portable pump and ensuring that the tubes connecting it to the patient did not become dislodged. This would have created an entirely new disaster, with blood spewing over the entire room! When Dr. Hayward entered the room and was appropriately gowned and gloved, he placed additional tubing into the groin area (at the top of the inner thigh) of the patient to have initial connection points for the larger pump. The larger pump setup had been completed using clear water solutions, so that the transfer from the smaller portable pump could be accomplished without disrupting flow to the patient's body.

No one was moving fast enough for Dr. Hayward. He had placed four towels around the chest area of the patient and screamed, "God dammit, where are the clamps?" Metal clamps were placed through the towels into the patient's skin, to ensure that the towels would not slip off. The scrub nurse on duty tonight was not his usual nurse and did not have things lined up on the table as Dr. Hayward was accustomed to seeing. One of his fellows reached over onto the table, retrieved the clamps and handed them to him. The scrub nurse's hands were visibly shaking as she handed off the larger sterile drape to completely cover the operative field. Dr. Hayward ripped the center tape from the drape to reveal the rectangular opening through which the operative procedure could occur. Fortunately, she had the appropriate scalpel to hand to him, and he sliced quickly into the patient's chest. Blood began to ooze around the area of the incision.

Dr. Hayward looked up and realized that I was at the head of the table. He then sneered, "The blood is awfully thin."

I replied, "As soon as the pump has some room, I will give him some blood."

The pump technician meanwhile had just begun to remove some of the excess water from the patient's blood through a filtration device that could leave blood and its components intact.

Hayward screamed, "Give him some blood now!"

I repeated, "I will give him some blood as soon as the pump has space for it."

He was livid and screamed, "God dammit. Get your ass out of here. When I want blood, I want it now!"

The rest of the room became so quiet that I'm sure you could hear a mouse piss on cotton!

Heads dropped and eyes were averted from Hayward's direction. It was as though they were certain that if found looking, he would immediately throw daggers into their eyes! I, of course, was in no mood to silently accept his abuse and continued my belligerent responses to him. What a change from the quiet, lady-like anesthesiologist who had started work there so many years ago.

I then screamed, "I will leave when another senior anesthesiologist comes to relieve me!" At that moment, the on-call anesthesiologist walked through the door.

As she came to the head of the table, Hayward screamed again, "Didn't I tell you to get your black ass out of here?"

I screamed back, "I will leave when I finish my report!"

It goes without saying that I was furious by this time. Since I had been on call the night before and had worked all night long, it was no picnic for me to be back in the operating room the very next night. As angry and hot as I was, I'm sure that I left a trail of smoke when I finally did leave the operating room. When I arrived home, I went immediately to bed because I knew that I was due back in the operating suite the next morning at 6:30 a.m. I had an extremely restless night.

The next morning, though I had not notified him, my chairman came over. The grapevine obviously travelled rapidly and overnight to alert the "powers that be" of the incident that had occurred between Hayward and me. My chairman came over to calm the situation down and was wearing his most diplomatic hat. He requested that Hayward and I should have a short meeting with him. This occurred in the hallway outside of the operating room!

"I recognize that patients over here are generally very sick and can often be thought of as having one foot in the grave and the other on a banana peel," said my chairman. His attempt at levity to lighten the situation went over like a lead balloon! "The anesthesiology and surgical teams over here are world renowned because you all are experts in this field. When we find someone who fits that bill, we like to keep the team intact. You two are part of this team and hopefully will have many days of successful patient outcomes. It is important to maintain your cool even in the most difficult circumstance. I hope that the two of you can put last night behind you and move forward," he stated.

There was a pregnant silence. I assumed that he was expecting some type of apology from us.

Neither of us apologized for the previous night's display, but we grudgingly agreed to continue working together. With that, the impromptu meeting ended. Naturally, whenever I worked with Hayward again, I felt that I was navigating a minefield!

After many, many, many years there and turnover of staff, Hayward began to slowly appreciate my expertise. I then became his "go to" person whenever he was faced with a problem during a case and the anesthesiology staff was junior to me. It was neither a joy nor a boost in confidence for me to be called to assist him. His outward affectations of friendliness were so disingenuous that I knew that I was only the better of two bad options in his mind.

While dealing with these multiple personality disorders in my professional life, I still had to maintain a good control of my home life for my husband and children. On the home front, life was under control. A sick child threw all of that control out of the window. Jai developed a severe case of asthma, requiring hospitalization. I called Dr. Nance to inform him of the situation and that I would not be able to come in. His response was, "We are kinda tight for coverage today and could really use your help. Since your daughter is in the hospital across the street, you should be able to come in for a while until the on call person arrives."

I couldn't believe my ears! I calmed myself before I spoke and said, "I'm sorry, but I won't be able to make it today. I have to go now, my baby needs me." I hung up. She was in the hospital for two days while they were adjusting her asthma meds, and I was there with her the entire time. Again, I realized that I had found my voice. No longer was the job the "be all – end all." My presence for family matters was more important!

Senior Surgeon Exhibiting Callous Indifference

Dr. Maurice Dunkirk

It appeared that unchallenged power had the capacity to ramp down malignancy to callous indifference! Such was the case with Dr. Maurice Dunkirk. He had as his front line several surgeons under him to do his front-line work and was not required to mingle with the masses in the operating room. I was definitely one of the masses and therefore rarely had the opportunity to work on his cases as a fellow; thus far, I had not worked on any as a faculty, either.

After my daughter's hospitalization, I returned to work and was on emergency night call. When I walked into the operating room, I saw that the only case going was one of Dr. Dunkirk's patients.

Dr. Dunkirk was world renowned in his ability to invent procedures and devices which could treat all diseases of the smaller vessels that supplied blood to the heart and brain. He was the pioneer of all things cardiac in nature, whether the use of leg veins to bypass the diseased vessels in the heart or neck or the invention of artificial hearts.

His patient population included heads of state from other countries and the super-rich of this country. His egomaniacal actions were demonstrated in other ways. His surgical rounds of patients occurred not on the ward but in his special room, where referring physicians of all specialties were in attendance to present their patients for consideration to be placed on his surgical schedule. No one could ride on the same elevator with him. Special coat hooks with his name engraved on them were strategically placed in the operating theater. All of his scrub attire had his name embroidered thereon. As a general rule, no one could provide the anesthetic care of his patients but the chief of the service or Dr. Willingham. In my early days there, he had four operating rooms designated for the care of his patients, with several younger associates to start the preliminary work on them. Of course, I was never assigned to take care of his patients.

Even though I was the faculty on call for the night, I was not allowed to take over the care of the patient as was the usual custom for the physician on call. This was the only case going on in the operating room that evening. My chief called Dr. Willingham in from home to relieve him and had me sit in the anesthesiology holding area while she finished up his case! I felt as useless as a tit on a boar hog. It was moments like this that threatened to drown my very soul.

My sense of self was sorely tested and was failing me. In spite of this, I survived.

I continued to put on a brave front for my children, who attended the same school as Dr. Dunkirk's child. At various school functions, he could be seen preening like a peacock whenever his child had played a part, no matter how miniscule. Though on occasion we were in close proximity, he looked right through me and never acknowledged my presence. I returned the favor and never acknowledged him either!

As with most situations, time has a way of changing things. Several years passed, and on this particular weekend, I was the faculty on weekend call. No cases were going on in the operating room. I was called at home and told that Dr. Dunkirk had a patient who needed a central line. I was amazed that a renowned surgeon such as he could or would not place a central line in one of his super-rich patients! Our anesthesiologists placed all central lines into patients for surgical procedures, allowing us to develop an unparalleled degree of expertise in such procedures. In other operating rooms in this hospital, only surgeons placed central lines. Obviously, my daily experience of central line placements over the years was now in the realm of acceptable!

I walked into the patient's room after having been paged four times in the span of twenty minutes and found Dunkirk and another very senior surgeon standing at the patient's bedside. I introduced myself to the patient and asked both surgeons to leave the room. Ahhh, self-confidence can taste as sweet as the nectar of the gods. A quivering, scared, old, rich man is just that – quivering, scared, and old. I used my superb bedside manner to put him at ease. Due to my level of expertise, I was able to perform the central line placement quickly and efficiently. Relief was evident on the faces of Dr. Dunkirk and his associate when I allowed them back into the room a few minutes later. They actually verbalized how much they appreciated my assistance!

My, my, how times had changed!

Though his international reputation continued as cardiac surgeon "par excellence," Dunkirk's appearances in the operating room became more and more infrequent. No longer were four rooms set aside just in case he needed one. In the event that he had a head of state or a celebrity, he would always escort them into the room, but after they were asleep, one of his former associates would perform the surgical procedure. This was the case the day before another natural disaster caused our hospital to shut down normal operations and revert to "emergency only" protocols.

Massive flooding occurred after a hurricane, wiping out all but minimal backup power. When I was able to safely get out of my house that morning and get to the hospital, I saw boy scouts lining the various stairwells with flashlights to provide illumination. Makeshift intensive care units had to be set up in areas previously designated as recovery rooms or triage rooms. Patients had to be hand-carried down these dimly lit stairwells on stretchers, regardless of weight. Those who were ventilator-dependent required multiple personnel to aid in their transfer. One person would have to breathe for them using an ambu bag and portable oxygen, while someone else had the responsibility of bringing down the machinery. If they required additional tubes, intravenous lines, and pressure monitors, other personnel had to be responsible for bringing all of that down. Some patients were transferred to other, undamaged parts of our hospital, but others had to be transported through connecting passageways to the professional building across the street.

It was in the midst of this chaos that his prima donna patient from the previous day decided to raise hell because he could not see Dr. Dunkirk and have his pain taken care of by Dr. Dunkirk himself. The patient had been transferred from his gilded VIP room, which now lacked power, to another area of the hospital which was far less inviting. The tantrum that he was putting on made it seem that another world war was about to erupt. He screamed at and insulted nursing personnel, residents, respiratory therapists, and anyone else who dared to walk into his room. He said that he was in pain, and Dr. Dunkirk was the only one who could take care of him. Dr. Dunkirk, unknown to him, had left town immediately after his surgery the previous day. One of the nurses saw my name on the anesthesiology record and called me so that I could be apprised of the situation.

When I walked in, he remembered me from the previous day. I feel certain that his memory was not of his pre-surgery frightened state! On the morning of surgery, I had assured him that he could hold on to his daughter's picture until he went off to sleep and that I would place it next to his head during the surgery. That, along with a huge dose of "Vocacaine," relaxed him enough. He then agreed to be taken to the operating room without being completely asleep. "Vocacaine" was something I had learned as a medical student. It was the ability to soothe a patient merely with your voice and mannerisms, without the use of drugs. Today, I knew that he would need more than "Vocacaine" to take care of his anxiety and post-surgical pain to bring him down out of the stratosphere! In spite of all of the chaos going on, I was able to obtain and administer the medications he needed to get the situation under control.

It took a while, but our hospital and our city recovered from the disastrous effects of the flood.

As Dr. Dunkirk aged, he took on more the role of elder statesman and less the expert surgical technician. He was frequently asked to appear and be honored or to speak at various functions. His presence in the operating room became a rare occurrence. Several years later, I had the opportunity to travel with him and a group of other physicians to commemorate the anniversary of a hospital in one of the South American countries. We were all speakers for the program held at that hospital. This was the first time in all the years that I had worked around him that I was truly impressed by Dr. Dunkirk. He gave a fascinating account of the history and evolution of surgery without using a single note for approximately one hour. At that time, he became human to me and obviously, I became human to him. He asked me on several occasions while we were in South America to take a picture of him with some of his patients who had been operated on as babies. He and I took a picture together to commemorate the anniversary also. After this, when I saw him around the campus of our own facilities, he spoke to me by name and engaged me in conversation! Sometimes, with age comes civility!

"Bullies by any name are still bullies." – Unknown

Senior Surgeons Exhibiting Appreciative Acceptance

Dr. Saul Levinsky

The remaining senior surgeons with whom I worked and labeled our professional relationship as appreciative acceptance were Dr. Saul Levinsky and Dr. Lynne Dunston.

Dr. Levinsky was a world-renowned aortic surgeon. He was sent patients from all over the United States and various parts of the world that other surgeons didn't have the expertise to even attempt to operate on for these difficult repairs. I remember hearing him belittle one of his patients who, in his pre-surgical nervousness, was questioning the procedure he was about to undergo and whether insurance would pay such an enormous cost. Levinsky was livid that someone had the audacity to question him!

Levinsky screamed, "I have invented or perfected this procedure and many others. No one can question me on the cost or how the operation will proceed. You have a fifty-fifty chance that you will live and a fifty-fifty chance that you will die! I don't know if I want to operate on you today or not!" With that, Levinsky turned and walked out of the room.

What an appalling display of egotistical bullying! It became so quiet in the room that one could probably hear a chinch bug fart! I don't know if the patient returned, but he certainly was not operated on that day.

In the early days of working with Levinsky, he too tried the scream-and-belittle approach on me for a little while. His primary scrub nurse took me aside after a couple of days of this and said, "Doctor, you must not hold your tongue. Stand up to him! Fight back, and tell him exactly what is going on! If you don't, he will constantly be on your case and will never trust you."

I followed her advice and became proactive in my approach to him. I would give reports on the patients before he had a chance to question me. Our working relationship eventually became great. He never hovered when I was starting a case anymore. Only his junior associates and residents were in the room. He made it a practice to come in only when it was time for him to perform his part of the operation.

In spite of my personal observation of his past bullying, I developed the utmost respect for his surgical skills and his work ethic. I was never the object of any of his rants any more. He was sorely lacking in social skills and exhibited such, even in professional meetings with his peers! He was purported to have welcomed a visiting Chinese surgeon by referring to him as a chink!

In the operating room, he was particularly taken by the speaking voice of one of our Hispanic techs, Romero. There was no trace of an accent when Romero spoke. When Dr. Levinsky would realize that he was in the room, he would say, "Say something, Romero." All the while he would be turning to everyone else saying, "Listen to that boy. He sounds like he went to Harvard or somewhere. Ain't that amazing?"

Levinsky was the epitome of the southern cracker who grew up with nothing and had now amassed a fortune. He had no social graces and obviously had missed the English classes that covered subjects and verbs!

He often commented on my earrings and how pretty they were. One day, he questioned, "Dr. Ruth, have you ever had a White boyfriend?"

I responded, "Yes, but my daddy threatened to disown me if I didn't get out of that relationship!"

He then responded, "Oh, so your daddy is the bigot!"

I said, "Yes, he would as soon spit on you as speak to you!" That ended that conversation!

On one particular evening, I had the responsibility for emergency night call. We had finished all the elective cases by 8:30 p.m., and I was able to go home. Jai was already in bed, but Eriela was still doing her homework. Jarrett had had an early day and was able to cook his famous "noodle-roni stroganoff" for the girls' dinner. After I arrived, the housekeeper retired to the guest room, where she stayed for the night since I was on night call. Jarrett went in to check on Eriela's progress with her homework, while I climbed into bed. I was praying that I would not be called back in, since I was slated to go the school for an honors program the next day. Unfortunately, it was not to be! The telephone rang at 2:00 a.m., and the operating room nurse informed me that Dr. Levinsky had a patient flying in who would arrive around 3:00 a.m. I got out of bed, dressed quickly, and was out of the house headed to the hospital.

Unlike many of the surgeons, when Dr. Levinsky was expecting a patient, he was in the operating room before the patient arrived. Therefore I knew that I, too, should be there before the patient arrived. It was a small case to us, an abdominal aortic aneurysm. At many other hospitals, it was considered a major case. After we started the case, Dr. Levinsky was able to finish the repair in forty-five minutes. I was back home and in my bed by 4:30 a.m. I was not interrupted the remainder of the night and was reasonably fresh when I attended the honors program at my daughter's school that morning.

When I returned to work after my post-call day, I saw that I was again scheduled to staff Dr. Levinsky's case. It seemed that we were becoming a matched pair.

He had booked a second-time redo chest (previously operated on twice) for a coronary artery bypass. One of his young associates had been tasked with the preparatory work of opening the chest and readying the patient for bypass. The structures in a chest that had previously been operated on were bound so tightly together that one would think glue had been placed inside the body. It was truly a delicate dance to release the heart and surrounding structures from these cement-like adhesions while maintaining the integrity of the heart and blood vessels. One wrong slip of the scissors or knife could result in a life-threatening hemorrhage for the patient. In addition, a heart that was compromised by blocked coronary arteries didn't have the same resiliency as a normal heart. Manipulations by the surgeon would continually depress cardiac function. Oxygenation would be severely impaired, resulting in decreases in all indices of cardiac function: mixed venous oxygen saturation, arterial saturation, cardiac output, and blood pressure. As the anesthesiologist, I was responsible for administering the appropriate fluids and medications to return the heart to reasonable function to attain stable vital signs. After two hours of painstakingly slow attempts to free the heart, we were still not ready for bypass, and the patient's heart was becoming less and less responsive to the various interventions that I was trying.

I made the decision that the senior surgeon, Dr. Levinsky, needed to be called to determine the best course of action. When he appeared, I apprised him of the situation. He immediately turned and went out to the scrub sink to clean his hands and arms. He returned to the room, hands up and dripping with water, and took the towel from the scrub nurse to dry them. She gave him a sterile gown, which he donned, and while allowing the circulator to tie it, the scrub nurse quickly placed a sterile glove on each of his hands. With that done, he quickly turned to the table and had the sternal saw placed in his hand. He zipped open the chest (breastbone) with the saw, requested heparin to be placed by the anesthesiology team, quickly placed the cannulas (tubing necessary to connect to a heart-lung machine), and placed the patient on bypass -- all in a span of three minutes!

He then looked at me and said, "How do you like that?"

I responded, smiling under my mask, "You can open my chest for bypass any day!"

Having developed a good working rapport with him, though the cases were stressful, I felt that I was gaining invaluable experience in the management of such patients.

On any number of occasions, some of his ascending aneurysm patients were blue and could barely breathe sitting in an upright position. They certainly could not be laid down, the usual position for sleep induction, prior to placing a breathing tube in the trachea. I found that Dr. Levinsky had obviously been in this situation many times before, and had a routine. He would come in with the patient, have the nursing staff prep and drape the patient for surgery, and place large catheters in the groin (upper thigh) vessels. This was done while the patient was awake. Medications to numb the area locally would be given to minimize pain and discomfort while the catheters were being placed. Prior to going on bypass, we had to ensure that the patient's blood would not clot, by administering heparin. Within seconds of bypass, I would put the patient to sleep, flatten the bed, place a breathing tube in his trachea, and connect him to a ventilator. Patients like this, with severely diminished cardiac status, required significant additional monitoring. These monitors were routinely placed into the heart by way of either the internal jugular vein or the subclavian vein. Because of the proximity to major arteries and the heart, risks of puncturing these vessels and the heart were always uppermost in my mind as possible complications that needed to be avoided at all costs. A hole in a major blood vessel of the neck, chest, or heart in a heparinized patient could lead to life-threatening bleeding. Consequently, these procedures were usually done prior to surgical exposure and institution of cardiopulmonary bypass. The critical nature of this patient required that surgery be started and cardiopulmonary bypass begun prior to the induction of anesthesia. Dr. Levinsky may have had his routine, but this situation had the potential to throw me completely out of mine!

I did not have time to ponder the order of things, as disconcerting as it was. Rapid processing and action were critical to the life of this patient. This was not a hands-on teaching moment for my resident! I quickly took control of my end of things, put the patient to sleep, and inserted all of the central monitors that were needed, in spite of his heparinized status. Having the patient on cardiopulmonary bypass, with the machine taking over the function of his heart and lungs, allowed the entire team to get everything else organized and proceed with the job of replacing his ascending aorta (the major artery that comes off of the heart to supply the body with blood).

It was reassuring to be able to work with a surgeon who had a plan regardless of the severity of the situation, and who was able to take charge in a quick and decisive manner. I learned that I, too, could successfully step up to the challenges of life-threatening situations with the same calmness and sense of purpose as Dr. Levinsky.

Dr. Lynne Dunston

If one focused on the continual malignancies and callous indignant behavior that I experienced, the question would arise: Why would any intelligent human stay in such a cesspool of malignant personalities? My answer: The cases were exciting! Such an adrenaline rush occurred when true emergencies appeared, especially with a surgeon such as Dr. Lynne Dunston, whose personality had not been tainted by the malignancies of the old guard.

The front desk would receive a call, "Please page Dr. Dunston to the cath lab." Two minutes later, the overhead speaker erupts again, "Anesthesia, cath lab number 3." This was rapidly followed by,

"Pump team, cath lab number 3." The last pronouncement in this sequence would be, "Room 1 nurses, call the front desk." After this pronouncement, everyone in the operating room had hit "Go Mode"!

Prepping for an emergency case brought operating room number one alive with the sounds of preparation. Rips, tears, and thuds of instruments hitting operating tables, anesthesia carts, and perfusion machines provided their own unique symphony of the impending emergency. Though the untrained eye of a bystander might see a chaotic mixture of people moving in disarray, the actuality was a well versed chorus of members whose individual parts came together to provide a symphony of lifesaving preparedness. The operating room was now in a whirl of preoperational energy.

Several nursing assistants were standing guard by the elevator door to help maneuver the bed and equipment of this patient, whose life was hanging by a thread, around the corners and into operating room one. Suddenly, the double doors swung open and revealed a patient connected to a lifesaving portable bypass pump, and monitoring equipment. The parade of people and equipment moved hurriedly into the operating room. Everyone knew what to do.

Hands materialized as my resident took the patient's head and barked, "One, two, three!" The patient was lifted quickly and gently into the air into the waiting arms of the operating crew and placed onto the crisp white sheets of the operating table. There was added tension to these initial preparatory steps because everyone knew of this patient's fragile cardiac status.

The cardiorespiratory portable monitors were disconnected and then reconnected to those required for surgery in the operating room. As the patient was being moved toward me in the air, I inserted a steel needle into his right subclavian vein, as evidenced by the spurt of blood in the attached syringe. While the patient was being settled on the table, I quickly placed additional central venous catheters and cardiac monitoring devices. The pulmonary artery pressures were very high, indicative of a failing heart. There was never a thought that this was an unmanageable situation for me.

Meanwhile, the circulating nurse was painting the chest with Betadine. Dr. Dunston, the surgeon, had done a quick scrub of his hands and arms. He was now donning gown and gloves, with the assistance of the scrub nurse. He and his assistant received the appropriate towels, clamps, and drapes from the scrub nurse and proceeded to cover the patient. Dr. Dunston gave a cursory look to the head of the table, as the scrub nurse handed him the scalpel to ensure that the patient was asleep prior to incision. I indicated with a nod that the patient was ready. My team and I had given the patient the appropriate medications for deep general anesthesia and anticoagulation to make sure that the patient's blood did not clot the tubing connecting him to the lifesaving cardiopulmonary bypass machine.

The scalpel sliced effortlessly through the skin and soft tissue above the breastbone. The circulating nurse had taken my place at the right shoulder of the patient so that the surgeon could hand off the connection for the saw. After connecting, she depressed the foot pedal and the whirring noise of the saw took over, as the patient's breastbone was smoothly split down the center. Spurts of blood began their dance around the edges of the breastbone, in an attempt to notify all concerned that the patient's tissues had been assaulted. Burning flesh was smelled as the surgeon used an electrical pen-like device known as a cautery to stop the flow of blood.

Snip, Snip -- scissors cut through the covering of the heart, known as the pericardium.

The pericardium was open, and the heart was lazily contracting, attempting to keep its job as primary circulator of blood.

Dr. Dunston said, "Is the heparin level okay?"

I said, "Yes."

He then placed a second large tube in one of the right chambers of the heart and secured it with a clamp, to keep the blood from coming out. After placing an additional tube in the aorta (the main artery supplying the body) and securing its initial clamp, he was now ready for the heart-lung machine to take over. As he unclamped both tubes, blood rushed down the right heart tube into the machine, mixing with the fluid that had been placed as a space holder. The fluid returning through the aortic tube rapidly changed from clear to pink to the deep red of the blood that had left the body.

A collective sigh could be heard in the room as everyone realized that this crucial phase had occurred without the patient going into cardiac arrest prematurely. Now the room could be left to the team necessary for the care of the patient from this point forward – surgeon plus one or two assistants, my team, perfusionists, scrub nurse, and two circulating nurses. Anyone else could be called in on a moment's notice. Dr. Dunston attached some veins from the patient's leg to the heart, successfully bypassing the blocked arteries. With the new blood flow supplying the heart, the patient came off the bypass machine without a problem and was settled into the intensive care unit at the end of the case.

Returning to the operating room and its chaos of blood-soaked sheets, bloody tubing, bloody instruments, and floor marked by pools of blood, I looked at the circulating nurse's chart and saw that from the time of entering the room to incision was exactly twelve minutes! I was left with the flush of success. My patient had been left in the care of the ICU team with stable vital signs!

Equanimity under duress!

My children were getting older and more involved in school activities. My husband and I tried to schedule as many vacation days as possible to fit their various field trips, athletic events, plays, and special days at school. We needed for them to feel that they were an important part of our lives. When the mommies were asked to help the kindergarten teacher by cutting out shapes and gathering material for the math class, I pitched in. Fortunately, I had developed better relationships with some of the anesthesiology faculty members, and while on breaks, they enthusiastically cut colored shapes for my daughter's kindergarten class, too! My baby was able to present her teacher with little plastic bags of material from her mommy, just as the other kids did. No one realized that these little bags had been provided by some of the highest-paid doctors in Houston!

We were also blessed to have been able to find a woman who was able to work a flex schedule for us. She took my children to school, picked them up, and stayed with them until one of us was home. Whenever I was on night call, she would sleep over, since we did not know when my husband would be called in to work. With advance scheduling, we were able to participate fully in our children's lives. On that front life was good.

25 - RETURN OF SELF-CONFIDENCE

<u>Spring – 1997</u>

As I was on my way to work this morning, I realized that my butt had lost the continuous nervous clench that had been my sidekick for so many years. My confidence level in my ability to handle anything that was thrown my way was at the highest level possible.

Maria, one of the operating room nurses, was passing by our office and said, "I see we are in the same room today."

"Really! Which room?" I replied.

"Room 8. Dr. Caliph is operating on Mr. Jonah today," she said. Dr. Caliph was actually one of the surgical fellows who had trained in this operating room during the same time as my training. He was one of the fortunate few who had been able to obtain a job there after completion of his training.

"Jonah. Where have I heard that name before?" I asked.

"He was the guy who arrested when Dr. Caliph was doing his right carotid last week!" she replied.

My butt clench returned, and my entire being appeared to have turned on a dime.

"I guess you drew the green weenie today!" she laughingly responded.

The "green weenie" is what we termed the worst set of circumstances, patients, and surgeon. Boy did I have it in spades! Not only was Mr. Jonah having his other carotid repaired today, but his thoracic aneurysm was to be taken care of, too. Our bodies have millions of blood vessels, all of different sizes and capacities. The aorta is the largest blood vessel that we have, and all of our blood goes through it to supply the nutrients necessary for life. If you can imagine a balloon expanding while being filled with water to its breaking point, you will have a good idea of how an aneurysm looks in the aorta. Further, if that balloon breaks, all of its contents are spilled out. The same would happen if an aneurysm broke, releasing all of the blood it contained. This would cause immediate death if it happened while you were driving down the street. In addition to the complexity of the surgery and the critical state of the patient in this case, my resident was brand new to our unit and very early in his training.

This is the tenuous situation into which I was now walking. I remembered the calls for help to that room when he went into cardiac arrest last week. Today, I would be taking care of him. The tension in my neck skyrocketed, and I reminded myself that I must maintain equanimity under duress. If the patient had arrested when they were previously operating on his neck, what was he going to do today when not only his neck but also his entire chest cavity was open and undergoing operative procedures? His previous procedure, when compared to today, would be like pissing in a hurricane!

I quickly put on my operating-room scrubs and went in to check the anesthesia area in the operating room that my resident had set up.

The anesthesia work area was located immediately behind the operating bed and at its head. This space contained a multilevel table with drawers and shelving, as well as a lockable cabinet against the wall. On the top shelf of the anesthesia workstation, numerous monitors were sitting with the ability to digitally read out various parameters, such as heart rate, oxygen saturation, and carbon dioxide and anesthetic gas levels. Three steel poles were attached to the table-back and were adorned with steel chambers, which held anesthetic agents in a liquid form which could be transformed into a gas vapor when needed. These gas vapors had the capacity to induce a total anesthetic state resulting in a pain-free, immobile, and deep sleep. Life-sustaining oxygen was piped into the table from a central supply hose hanging from the ceiling, but in an emergency, could be given from the green cylinders that were attached to the back of the table. The ventilator was strategically placed at the front side of the table, to allow ease of access when attached through disposable tubing to the patient. The white crystals through which all of the patient's gases flowed were checked to ensure that no lavender color was peeking through, indicating that they had used their full capacity for absorbing and thus removing the carbon dioxide.

An array of syringes was lined up in layers on the table. Potent narcotics for pain relief, sedative hypnotics for sleep induction, and muscle relaxants for paralysis filled the normal-use syringes. Medications to speed up the heart, increase its ability to contract, and suppress irregular rhythms were just a few of the fillings for the emergency syringes. Several steel free-standing poles were adjacent to the command pressure platform and had individual pumps attached, which could provide continuous infusions of medications when needed.

The cabinet contained drawers of sterile replacement dressings, syringes, needles, tubing, and fluids. After noting that my resident had prepared everything correctly, I left the room.

I went in to speak with Mr. Jonah and saw that Bill, the electrophysiology technician, was in the final stages of attaching electrodes to his scalp. These would allow us to keep abreast of his brain wave activity during the surgical procedure.

I walked over and said to Bill, "Did your son's team win last night?"

He smiled and replied, "No, Doc. I hope that they will win a game before he graduates!"

Mr. Jonah interjected, "My son's college team is struggling to win, too. I had hoped that he would get noticed by a college scout and receive some perks to help with all of my bills, especially with the amount you are charging to put me to sleep, Doc."

I laughingly replied, "You are not paying me to put you to sleep. My charge is for waking you up!"

Fortunately, my resident had been able to place the appropriate catheters in Mr. Jonah's artery and vein. We would use the arterial catheter for blood pressure monitoring and the venous catheter for medication injection.

Each room had two circulating and one scrub nurse. The circulating nurses would be the ones who could bring any additional equipment or summon any additional personnel needed during the operative procedure. The scrub nurse would be clad in sterile gown and gloves to assist the surgeon. All three of the nurses had been parading in and out of operating room eight with sterile packs. They selected and brought in the blue-paper-covered packs of sterile instruments, containers, and gowns. For anyone in the room, the snap, drag, and tear of the tape holding the paper together could be heard periodically, heralding the readiness of the paper to give up its sterile contents. After appropriately draping the table that would hold all of the operative instruments, the scrub nurse would go outside to the scrub sink, don a mask, and appropriately cleanse arms and hands with bactericidal soap. Upon returning to the room, the nurse would don gown and gloves in a sterile fashion, with the assistance of the circulating nurse. They would then count and document every needle, scalpel, sponge, and instrument that had been placed on the table in preparation for surgery. With all of that accomplished, Maria, one of the circulating nurses, would be able to let us know when the patient could be brought into the room.

Maria walked into the holding area and said to Mr. Jonah, "We are ready for you in the operating room. I see that you have the 'A' team taking care of you today!"

He laughingly replied, "You mean that you all have 'B' teams here, too? I'll remember in the future to always request the 'A' team!" After this short banter, I slowly injected a short-acting sedative hypnotic into his vein and saw the visible relaxation that it provided.

With that, we took up positions at the head and side of the bed and began to wheel Mr. Jonah down the hall to operating room number eight.

Room 8 was its own self-contained pod. Built-in cabinets encompassed three walls of the room. They contained a myriad of gloves, needles, dressings, drapes, and containers which could be called into action at a moment's notice. A stereo system was discreetly housed in the back corner and available for country western tunes, the preference for most of the surgeons. The operating table stood at attention in the center of the room, with its white sheet crisply folded at the corner with military precision. The table was perched atop a gleaming silver multi-tiered base and locked into place with four steel footplates.

Bill followed closely behind us and wheeled in the equipment that would be used to monitor Mr. Jonah's brain waves. He and his machine took up their position in the left corner of the operating room, toward the head of the operating bed.

We wheeled the bed snugly against the operating table and asked Mr. Jonah to slide over. I gave support to his head as he sleepily slid from the wheeled cart to the operating bed. Everyone except the senior surgeon, Dr. Caliph, was in attendance. His resident and fellow were standing there in his stead.

The monitoring technician was standing by to help with the transfer of all catheters and eventually connect them to the devices that would show us digital readouts of the patient's vital signs. The monitoring platform command post for these pressure parameters stood immediately to the left back of the operating table. A large television-like monitor hovered above this command post and communicated blood, central venous, and pulmonary artery values via high pressure tubing connections.

Maria and I gently tucked Mr. Jonah's arms alongside his body under a folded bedsheet. We began our process of anesthesia induction as my resident placed an oxygen mask over his nose and mouth to increase the amount of oxygen flowing through his body. Within minutes of the pre-oxygenation procedure, narcotics and stronger sedative hypnotics wound their way through his bloodstream and induced a deep anesthetic sleep. Even though the procedure on his neck was to be done first, we had to place all of the appropriate endotracheal tubes and monitors needed for the second procedure.

My resident placed a double lumen endobronchial tube into his trachea, so that we would have the ability to deflate the left lung while leaving the right lung inflated during the thoracic portion of the procedure. I recognized the increased complexity of placing an internal jugular vein catheter in the neck of someone who had previously undergone a surgically repaired carotid artery. I chose not to have the resident put in the central lines and placed them myself. I had the added burden of knowing that there was no room for error; a mistake could lead to the loss of the one lung we would have available to us during the thoracic portion of the procedure. The circulating nurse placed a Foley catheter and temperature monitoring device in his bladder, while we busied ourselves at the head of the patient. With everything done and all the monitors now connected, the patient's left neck and shoulder area could be washed and cleaned with Betadine solution. Everything was now ready for the surgical procedure to begin.

The surgeon, Dr. Caliph, entered the room with his entourage, and they were all appropriately gowned and gloved. He stepped to the side of the table, looked at me, and barked,

"How's he doing?"

"He's stable," I replied.

This verbal exchange was shortcut language directed at determining vital signs, life functions, and problems. My answer, while not giving specific numbers, was my considered assessment of the patient's blood pressure, pulse rate, heart function, and oxygenation. There was a certain added tension to our interchange because we both knew of the fragile cardiac status of this patient.

The procedure itself was so routine and well known to the surgeon and scrub nurse that they could begin with little to no verbal communication. He reached out one hand, and she deftly placed his preferred scalpel into it. As he gently sliced into the side of the patient's neck, blood made a tiny leap upward but was immediately squelched by sponges and a Bovie cauterizer, which was now in Dr. Caliph's hand. I noted a slight rise in blood pressure and administered a small dose of narcotic, which brought it back down. Dissecting and exposing the left carotid artery went on without a problem. A shunt was placed into the artery during the procedure so that there would be no interruption in blood supply to the brain.

The patient continued to do well, and there was no further blood pressure or heart rate change. After the carotid patch was completed, the shunt removed, and the neck sewn up, we all breathed a collective sigh of relief that there was no arrest of the heart, as had occurred last week.

The next stage required that the patient be turned onto his side with his right chest down, a shoulder roll under his chest, and his left arm secured in a right-angle, towel-draped metal sling over his face. After appropriate positioning and securing of all catheters, the patient's chest and abdomen were scrubbed with Betadine. Sterile towels and drapes were reapplied to cover his body. Dr. Caliph and his team rescrubbed their arms and hands and reentered the operating room. After new sterile gowns and gloves were on, Dr. Caliph stepped to the left side, at the head of the operating bed. His resident and fellow were positioned on the right side of the bed. The scrub nurse, standing on a footstool, was at Dr. Caliph's left, toward the feet of the patient. The table of instruments, now waist-high for the scrub nurse, was perched above the patient's legs. Dr. Caliph again turned to me and asked,

"How is he doing?"

I again replied, "Stable."

I heard the crisp snap of the scalpel from the nurse into the surgeon's hand. I then saw the steel scalpel fly with laser precision, slicing effortlessly through the aorta. Blood leapt into the air and spewed into the operative field, as suction catheters slurped and sucked, forcing it back into the Cell Saver to preserve its lifesaving properties. The Cell Saver machine was always at the ready, to the right of the anesthesia table. The Cell Saver technician was also prepared to begin the process of separating the blood from its components, so as to be able to return it to the patient when needed. He had connected one of its tubes into a large catheter that had been placed into the patient's neck. Pressure parameters began a slow downward spiral, necessitating pharmacological and fluid resuscitation of the patient's vital signs. My assistant and I were in constant motion as we sped up the dance of fluid replacement, drug infusions, and bolus injections. Suddenly I noticed that the expected response was not occurring, and the blood pressure began a downward death spiral.

"Dr. C., he is beginning to decompensate," I said.

He looked up at me and barked loudly,

"I have the aorta wide open! What do you expect me to do?!"

"Sew fast," I responded.

My brain, eyes, and hands kicked into overdrive as I determined which medications and fluids should receive their marching orders.

"Get me another pair of hands in here," I screamed to the nurse.

My resident became paralyzed with his inexperience and began moving slower as I sped up. The Cell Saver tech had the machine going full out, processing the blood returning from the operative field and rushing back into the patient's large bore central catheter.

The heart stopped beating. My last interchange with Mr. Jonah ran fleetingly across my brain.

"You pay me to wake you up!"

The surgeon gave three mighty squeezes to the heart, followed by intermittent suturing of the graft. This dance continued for several minutes. I continued to rapidly provide fluid and medications to normalize blood pressure and heart function. Their current values were threatening to put a death grip on this patient.

The brain waves were slowing to a crawl.

The surgeon and I were the only ones in flat-out, full-speed-ahead motion. Everyone else in the room seemed to have gone into slow motion as they anticipated the end.

The last suture went into the graft.

"Head down," the surgeon barked.

The mechanics of the table allowed me to place the patient such that his feet were in the air and his head was lowered toward the floor.

The surgeon slowly began the removal of the aortic clamp. The acid load from the non-perfused bottom portion of the body rushed up and forced the blood pressure down further. I counteracted rapidly with reversal meds and fluids, and the heart began a slow chaotic rhythm. Brain waves began to pick up. The heart was now dancing to its own beat.

I now began checking cardiac index and other indices of cardiac function. Everything was slowly beginning to return to baseline, including the brain waves. Blood clotting parameter results were brought in by the tech and revealed a need for more platelets, plasma, and cryoprecipitate. The urine showed it telltale blue color, indicating the successful passage of dye through the kidneys. Urine output began to pick up and allowed me to get rid of some of the excess water that I'd had to give him, which helped stabilize his pressures. Bleeding from the operative field slowed enough for Dr. Caliph to feel confident that the surgical wound could be closed without fear of internal bleeding.

Dr. Caliph's resident and fellow finished the closure, placed chest tubes inside the chest, applied appropriate dressings, and prepared the patient for transference to the intensive care unit.

In the intensive care unit, I stood to the side as my resident gave his report to the nursing and medical team who would take over the patient's care. Fatigue, both mental and physical, was rapidly setting in for me. I was pleased to note that my name had a check mark beside it, indicating that I was free to go home after this exhausting six-hour procedure.

The intensity of that case should have left me totally drained and on edge, but it didn't. My professional expertise had reached a superior level of functioning. This allowed me to manage a case like this without the emotional drain that accompanied the end of similar cases early in my career.

I would later learn that Mr. Jonah had been discharged home after ten days with no mental deficits. One of my nurses termed it as being able to sell pencils and count change!

26 - NIGHT AND DAY EMERGENCIES

Night call should have been more aptly called day-and-night call because the hours stretched and spanned both day and night, especially when this duty occurred on the weekend. Transplant surgeries made up the lion's share of middle-of-the-night cases. This was the case, early in my career, with my first young donor, a young man who had become so drunk that he fell off of a twelfth-story balcony and was declared brain dead at the age of twenty. As he lay there in the ICU with stable vital signs, while preparations were being made to harvest his organs and tissues, I went to his bedside and talked to him. Though his sleep was of no tomorrow, he appeared to be as vibrant as one of my own similarly aged nephews, who also could be foolishly endangering themselves with their sense of immortality.

I touched him and said, "If there is any way that you can move an eyelid or finger, please do it now so that we won't end your life."

I sat with him for a few minutes until the orderlies arrived to take him into the operating room. With the first slice of the knife through his chest, my own chest rebelled, and I could not breathe. I had to run out of the room to keep others from seeing the floodgate of tears opening in my eyes. Fortunately, I rarely had to witness organ donations from young people and never again from one who had allowed alcohol to take over his senses.

My emotions always ran high during transplant cases. For a very long time, I questioned the parameters used to determine when the end of life necessary for organ donation had arrived. I am certain that a lot of it was due to the different outcomes of both of my parents so many years ago. Even though a physician had counseled that my mother should no longer remain on a ventilator, a part of me had always felt that he had been wrong. Even though my daddy arrested in front of me and remained comatose for two months, he still lived many years after that event. This lead to my "never give up on a patient" attitude!

Our operating suite was witness to many well-known dignitaries and celebrities from around the world, but there was a different air in the room if it happened to be a family member of one of their own. Such was the case when the mother of one of the surgeons, Josh, had to undergo coronary artery bypass surgery. Her heart had suffered major damage from her previous heart attacks and was severely weakened. After she was put under anesthesia and was being prepped for the surgery, her heart gave up its fight for life and stopped.

Even though the room had been adequately prepared for a routine bypass case, a different flurry of activity began in the room after her heart stopped. Additional anesthesiology, perfusion, and nursing personnel were paged stat to the room. These additional personnel would speed up the readiness for what now was an emergency procedure. External paddles used to shock the heart through a closed chest had their sterile coverings ripped off. Bags of drugs that made the heart pump more forcefully were removed from their packaging and placed in infusion pumps. Dosages were dialed into the pump so as to be used with the touch of a finger when needed.

Her surgeon, Dr. Blake, was paged stat to the operating room. He ran in asking what had happened.

I said, "She flatlined."

At this time, all efforts were being made to cleanse the body for surgery while one of the surgical fellows did chest compressions to take the place of the non-functioning heart. Dr. Blake quickly scrubbed, gowned, and gloved in order to prepare Josh's mother for the lifesaving bypass machine. Josh came into to the room and stood at the head of the table and whispered into his mother's ear, "You are going to be alright, Mom." My mind briefly reminded me of my own daddy's resuscitation at my hands and brought back the emotional dread of an impending loss of a loved one. Even though the socioeconomics of the patients and available technology were different, the emotional upheaval of seeing your mother lying on a bed dying were the same for Josh and me.

Dr. Blake was handed the sternal saw used to cut through the breast bone. A slit into the thin covering on top of the heart revealed a sluggish heart, lazily moving with no apparent force behind its movement. Appropriate tubing was placed into the heart for attachment to the heart-lung machine. As blood and water began mixing during their journey from the heart to the machine, the blood pressure on the monitor started to rise. At least for the moment, we knew that blood and oxygen were providing their life-giving function to the rest of her body.

The roar of emergency preparation was now dulled into a quiet hum. Veins would be harvested from the legs and subsequently attached to the heart. Several hours later, all vein bypass grafts had been attached. The moment had arrived to test the effectiveness of the restored blood flow to the heart. The aortic cross-clamp was removed to allow blood to flow through the vein grafts. The heart responded by going into a generalized, disorganized quivering. Internal paddles were used to provide an electric shock to the heart, which would interrupt these signals that it was receiving. After the shock, the heart began its lazy slow contractions, similar to those seen prior to the surgery. I decided to allow it to rest for a period of time from its no-blood-flow state prior to starting the infusion of medications to assist in its contractions. The heart began slowly improving in contractile appearance. When the decision was made to transfer the entire load of pumping blood through the body from the machine to the heart, the blood pressure went down and the numerical indices of heart function went up, indicating a failing heart. Even though small volumes of blood were transferred to the heart so that it could slowly become accustomed to the load, it failed each time with only half of its capacity. Each time this happened, we went back on full cardiopulmonary bypass support to rest the heart. Early that evening, Dr. Blake made the decision to use a mechanical left heart assist device. The on-call anesthesiologist came in to relieve me so that I could go home.

Burdened by the emotional drain of a child fearing for his mother's life, the intellectual drain of appropriate medication and fluid scenarios, as well as the physical strain of standing all day, I was thoroughly exhausted when I arrived home. Fortunately, my husband and children had already had their dinner. I had nothing left to give and fell immediately into bed!

When I arrived at work the next morning, I saw that Josh's mother was still in the operating room! All manner of mechanical heart assist devices had been tried during the previous evening and night, but with no success. Her heart was too fragile to take over its job. A number of surgeons were sitting in the doctors' lounge discussing the negative turn of events surrounding Josh's mother.

One of them decided to call The City hospital trauma chief for help: "We need a heart. Whatever comes through the door next, take it. We have to do whatever it takes to help her survive."

Willie Joe was privy to part of this conversation. He sought me out later in the morning, and with an alarmed look on his face said,

"Doc, dey in there talkin 'bout takin somebody's heart over at The City hospital for dat doc's momma layin in duh room!"

I tried quieting his fears of a "snatch and grab" scenario by saying, "They mean that they are putting her on the transplant list. They wouldn't kill anyone just to have a heart!" He appeared reluctantly satisfied with my response and said, "I'll keep my ears open jes in case. I don't want you gittin in no trouble!"

Five days later, the stench of human decay permeated the air in that operating room. Josh's mother had lain on that operating table for the entire week. Every anesthesiologist and nurse in the unit had participated in this, the latest waste of resources both human and material, because of the power of the cardiothoracic surgery department. Josh, once a rising star in cardiothoracic surgery, had been reduced to a grieving little boy who could not let his mother go. The cocksure senior surgeons for whom he had worked thirty-six-hour call every other night in his five-year quest to become a cardiothoracic surgeon assured him that they would take care of his mother. After all, they had access to all the latest technology in mechanical assist devices for the human heart, as well as donors coming through The City hospital's emergency room. They had already found two hearts for her this week! Fortunately, by Sunday, even the mighty realized they could not win this battle and stopped all attempts to save Josh's mother's life.

27 - WINSTON – SOCIOPATHIC ANESTHESIOLOGIST

Having navigated the minefields of old and new surgeons, as well as the shenanigans of various anesthesiology faculty, I had finally seemed to have earned my place as a competent member of the anesthesiology faculty. None of the previous malignancies seemed insurmountable until N. J. Winston became chief of the cardiac anesthesia team. He quickly alienated all but his trusted inner circle of two anesthesiologists and two surgeons in the unit. One of his first tasks was to try to send me, one of the most senior cardiac anesthesiologists on staff at this point, to work in the general operating room! I accepted the task without question, but I began writing letters to the senior administrators of the College of Medicine to apprise them of the deteriorating situation Dr. Winston was orchestrating. Amazingly, my stint in the general operating room lasted only two days! He continued to wreak havoc for approximately a year, at which time I had had enough. Paranoia was so great that it was rumored that Winston had installed spy camera and listening equipment in all of the faculty offices! I requested and received a meeting away from the hospital grounds with the chairman of our department, to discuss the major upheaval that Dr. Winston was causing.

On Saturday morning, my chairman and I met at a Starbucks café away from the hospital. I was fifteen minutes early and ordered coffee, which I normally did not drink. When my chairman arrived, I launched into a laundry list of all of the indignities and injustices that

Winston was causing among the faculty. Winston unapologetically switched assignments to ensure that junior residents were assigned to the most difficult cases, after having maligned the anesthesiologist of record to the operating surgeon. His intent was to stir up the surgeons and have them request removal or firing of faculty that were not loyal to him. He covered for his inner circle which, on occasion, came to work with alcohol on the breath. After a tongue-in-cheek praise of one faculty member in a meeting, Winston invited said faculty member out to lunch and stated that the faculty would be fired within the month. It was Winston's suggestion that the faculty member resign to save themselves from embarrassment! Even though the number of faculty was decreasing, Winston took himself out of the night call sequence and would only work with one surgeon, using the most senior of the junior personnel regardless of the simplicity of the case. It was also rumored that he was diverting departmental funds for his personal use. After my short monologue, my chairman said that he was beginning to realize that it had been a mistake to bring Dr. Winston there, but that he had no one to replace him. In my naiveté, I told him that I would be willing to replace Winston on a temporary basis until he could perform a national search to find someone permanent. Little did I realize that it would take more than a few months to find someone to replace me! He wanted to have the weekend to think this over, and I agreed. On Monday morning, he called me in and told me that he would take me up on my offer. I calmly agreed, but my heart began racing like a fire engine headed for a three-alarm fire.

That afternoon, the chairman called Dr. Winston and asked him to come over for a brief meeting. When he walked through the door, you could see the questioning surprise on his face that I would be in on a meeting with him and the chairman.

"What's this all about?" questioned Dr. Winston.

"Have a seat," said the chairman. "I have decided that we need to make some changes in the unit. You are an excellent anesthesiologist, and I value your work. I hope that you will continue to work in the cardiac unit, but I am installing Ruth as the acting chief."

Dr. Winston stammered, "When is this going to be effective?"

The chairman said, "Immediately."

Dr. Winston asked, "Can't you give me a few days to wrap up some things before you announce this?"

The chairman said, "No, we are calling a faculty meeting this afternoon to make this announcement." We stood up, and the meeting was over! As I was leaving the office suite, I heard the chairman instructing his secretary to contact all faculty members and inform them of the meeting that would occur in one hour that afternoon. My head was swirling with the enormity of the situation that I was now in. On my walk back to the operating room, I encountered the Senior Vice President for Educational Affairs of the College of Medicine. I told him about the events that had just transpired. He said, "It is about time that he was relieved of that job. If you need anything, just call me." It relieved some of the tension that I was feeling, knowing that I had support at one of the highest levels of the college of medicine.

My "brief time" as interim chief stretched into a year and a half! It was as though I had been transported back in time so as to relive first-hand all the warnings I had been given about the surgeons and anesthesiologists at this cardiac unit. My friend Willie Joe had become the "personal assistant" for the surgeons' lounge. He was a nonentity as far as they were concerned, and they spoke freely around him. He was privy to many conspiratorial conversations that occurred in the lounge, and he always found a way to inform me! This became extremely important during my tenure as interim section chief.

At every turn, I was being challenged by Dr. Winston, one of the other faculty, some of the surgeons, and another private group which wanted to take over the very lucrative cardiac anesthesia practice. I was scheduled to meet with representatives of the private group two or three times per week, so as to try to work out some type of mutually beneficial working relationship. Half the time, their representative would not show up for these 6:00 a.m. meetings! This exercise in futility ended up being a colossal waste of my time and energy, as no agreement was ever worked out.

I was continuing to do cases, take the same night call as other faculty members, and run the business of the section. Willie Joe continued to bring tidbits of information from conversations that he heard in the surgeons' lounge. Though not a surgeon, Dr. Winston was busy instigating ways to make me look bad in the surgeons' eyes. After a while, this resulted in a letter of "no confidence" to my chairman. I had relieved him of a significant burden by taking over the position. Regardless of their feelings, he was not about to relieve me of this dastardly duty! The plan was to start a search for a permanent section chief immediately. I don't know which steps were taken immediately, but I do know that when he came to me offering the job on a permanent basis, I all but screamed a resounding NO!

28 - JOBIE'S ILLNESS

Though I had become more comfortable with my professional work life, everything seemed to have gone askew when my sister became seriously ill. My sister Jobie, in Tennessee, required surgery for a pancreatic tumor. I spoke with my sister's surgeon, and with her permission, he informed me of her medical condition and assured me that he did not expect the tumor to be malignant. I was told that the procedure should be straightforward and done in a couple of hours. No alarms went off in my mind because my professional life was consumed with medicines and numbers: blood pressure, heart rate, blood gases, hematologic values, and chemistries of the blood. Usually, a surgeon had a reasonable idea of the length of time that a procedure would take. Therefore, "a couple of hours," in my mind, should not be long even if another forty-five minutes to an hour was tacked on. This would later prove to be an incorrect assumption on my part.

In critical times, surgeons would ask, "How's the patient doing?"

My response would be, "Doing well" or "Stable."

These pronouncements were always based on the "numbers," which were constantly being manipulated with anesthetic drugs, pharmacological agents, or various fluid products. Death in the operating room was a rarity. Vital signs could be made "stable"!

On the day of surgery, I flew to Tennessee to be with my sister and went directly to the hospital. She lay dozing in the sterile-looking hospital room, and Squeaky had her customary post at the side of the bed watching over her little sister, Jobie.

As I walked in, Jobie stirred and said, "You all don't need to be here." I told Squeaky that she could go, but I was staying. I knew the enormity of the surgical procedure that Jobie was about to undergo and felt that I should be there during surgery and when it was finished.

Instead of the previously mentioned "couple of hours," the surgery took nine and a half hours! The surgeon gave me the "professional courtesy" to send out periodic updates. At the conclusion of surgery, the surgeon came out and reported that everything had gone well and that her "vital signs were stable." He further stated that he would place her in I.C.U. as a "precautionary measure" since the surgery had gone "a little longer" than expected with significant fluid shifts.

I stayed until the third day post-surgery, at which time Jobie was transferred out of the ICU. This was the beginning of a nine month journey plagued by many complications -- paralysis, sepsis (blood infection), lung and kidney failure. I was traveling back and forth between Texas and Tennessee every three to four weeks to check on Jobie and speak with the healthcare team. Jobie was not improving.

My tenure as section chief was also taking its toll on me. I began losing weight, and the strain of it all was showing in my face.

Depression set in, not only for Jobie but for me too. She lashed out at all her loved ones, who were going to the hospital on a daily basis to help support her. My guilt for not sharing this time more frequently with them was all consuming. In spite of my family's constant vigilance over Jobie, they still tried to assuage my guilty feelings about my absence.

Jobie was sent to a nursing home six months after her initial surgery, without ever having been able to go home. We were not given sufficient notice to make preparations for her to leave the hospital and return home with a professional care team in place. Two weeks after her arrival in the nursing home, we were informed of infections that were raging rampantly among the nursing home population. Her immediate surroundings as well as the hallway were further impacted by her roommate's continuous diarrhea with its putrid odor. With this confluence of issues, there was no other room available to which she could be transferred. Room deodorizers and flowers were no match for those odors. After a while the overall situation was finally brought under control, but Jobie's depression affected her entire being. She began developing extremely painful bedsores in her lower back. The staff was tasked with cleaning and dressing them, another extremely painful event for my sister. Their technique was not very good and the infection began to spread.

We contacted another surgeon, who agreed to return her to the hospital to try to clean up the sores in hopes of closing them with skin grafts. While these discussions were going on and prior to her move back to the hospital for surgery, her vital signs became unstable. She was immediately transferred from the nursing home to the I.C.U. This began a cascade of organ system failures – lungs, kidneys, heart. I flew home. We had a family conference, and I was tasked with making all medical decisions. The next 72 hours proved to be critical ones due to the downward spiral that she was in. Her blood pressure was too low to undergo dialysis to get fluid out of her lungs. Her heart was failing in its ability to maintain enough flow to push fluid through her system. Her kidneys had long since given up their ability to work correctly. I sat beside her bed and started talking to her about what she was facing as she struggled to breathe through the CPAP ventilatory mask.

I took it off for a second, and she mouthed, "Help me." Her face was contorted with pain.

What "help" was she asking for? Did she want freedom from pain? Did she want a better way to breathe? Was the work of living getting to be too much for her? I felt that the world was crashing down on my shoulders and impairing my own ability to breathe. I requested that she be given more pain medicine and watched her drift off to sleep.

It was time to confer with her health care team about options and since this was the weekend, it was difficult to get in touch with them. One by one I was able to confer with the on call doctors whose opinions were that there were no other options available to help her and that everything had been done that could be done. I decided that I needed to review her lab work, "numbers," chest X-rays, and medical chart. After my own personal assessment and hearing their words reverberating in my head, I made the most difficult decision of my life. My sister should be taken off ventilatory support and made comfortable for her remaining time on earth.

A sense of overwhelming impotence invaded my body. After so many years of education and medical practice, I could do nothing to save my sister. How could this be? Though I was the youngest, she often turned to me for help both emotional and financial. I had become someone she could count on. Now I had failed her.

I put on my "professional face" and sent everyone home. After they left, tears rained down my face as my sorrow deepened at the prospect of the inevitable. I sat by her bedside for several hours before composing myself enough to be able to go home and face my family after such a colossal failure. After the pain medicine took over and she appeared to be resting comfortably, I left the hospital.

At 5:45 a.m., the call came that Jobie's heart rate was getting very slow. Jobie's daughter, sisters, and brother assembled around her bed. We talked to her to let her know that we were there with her. We held her hands and caressed her forehead as she took her last breath. My sister no longer had vital signs.

29 - OVERSEAS TEACHING PROGRAM IN AFRICA

A short time after Jobie's death, a new section chief for anesthesiology had been appointed, and I was relieved of my interim status. I thought that this would give me a break. Silly me! When the new chief came in, she turned the unit upside down and decided that several faculty members should do cases alone, without the benefit of residents or nurse anesthetists. And who was the first one to be given this task? I was, of course. I spent several days of my week going in early to set up and prepare for cases, as I had done as a fellow! Again, I gave no complaints. Even though other faculty members were given these assignments, it was quite demeaning and tiring for me to be treated as a fellow again!

In reading an anesthesiology journal, I saw an advertisement for the Overseas Teaching program in Africa. I applied to the American Society of Anesthesiologists (ASA) and was accepted. It took a bit of arm-twisting by the chairman and another section chief for my chief to allow me to go. I did receive the appropriate permissions and was preparing to go to Africa, with a colleague from a different institution, to teach cardiac anesthesia. Unfortunately, six weeks before we were to leave, he notified the ASA that he could not go! I had not planned to spend the full three months there and decided to compress my lecture series into three weeks.

The time to depart arrived and here I was again, traveling to a distant land alone! Traveling from Houston to Africa by way of Amsterdam took approximately eighteen hours. What a relief to finally feel the touchdown of the plane's wheels to the earth at 9:00

p.m. in Accra, Ghana. The night was a pleasant, humid one, not unlike those I felt as a child in Memphis. Chaos was rampant at the airport, with people disembarking from both the front and back doors of the plane. Adding to the chaos were cars driving up to the door of the plane to retrieve some important dignitaries. I soon found out that the public was not allowed inside the airport. Fortunately, the ASA had arranged for my contact, Perry, to carry an American flag as I carried a Texas flag by way of recognition. We met briefly, and he gave meeting instructions to me before going back outside. In the baggage claim area, the chaos continued. A porter walked up to me and told me that he would help with my bags.

As I was pointing them out, he started saying, "Give me some money."

I said, "I don't have any African money."

He persisted with darting eyes saying, "You have to give me some money quickly. Give me American money!"

At this point we were moving rapidly toward the outside, where throngs of people were crowded at the fence that separated the incoming passengers from those who were greeting them. My anxiety level was reaching code-red status, since I could not see anyone that I recognized. This man who was rolling all of my bags in an unknown direction constantly demanded money from me! I then spied my flag-waving contact on the periphery and virtually pulled my baggage cart from the man as I began moving, pushing and shoving, toward my contact. Fatigue, chaos, and fear began to totally consume my partially functioning brain. Perry helped me with the cart, and we made it to the minivan that was waiting, where we then unloaded the entire luggage cart.

My daughter had coined the phrase "Hard Dark" once when we were driving down some dark mountainous roads in North Carolina without the benefit of either moon or starlight. The streets that we were traveling on at this moment in Africa appeared even darker and more sinister than that to me! None of the buildings had lights in them, and there was an occasional street fire with figures huddled around it as we passed. After a one-hour drive, we made it to the Dean's guest house to retrieve the keys for the house that I was to stay in, at the bottom of the hill. I had spoken with my husband while in Amsterdam, and we planned that he would call me on Monday at 6:00 p.m. local time.

There was a metal gate with locks on the outside allowing entry into the main area of the house that I was to reside in during my stay. We passed through the locked door to gain entry into the foyer, which revealed doors to my room and another bedroom. Upon opening my bedroom door, I saw a twin bed draped in a long, white, filmy mosquito net; a small desk and chair in the corner; and a wall of windows covered with heavy maroon drapes. There was a bathroom with a toilet, sink, and shower, as well as a walk-in closet. I didn't have the energy to unpack a bag, so after ensuring that all the locks were in place, I merely flopped my fully clothed body across the bed and went to sleep.

I initially awakened around 3:00 a.m., but my body was still tired so I continued to lie there, drifting in and out of wakefulness. I dreamed that I had turned around and left immediately, without seeing anyone at the hospital! Imagine my surprise when I jumped out of bed at noon and found that I was still in Ghana, with no Jarrett, Eriela, or Jai! I used bottled water to brush my teeth and wash my face. Then I turned on the shower, but the water remained frigid in spite of knob adjustments to get it to warm. In addition to that, a big brown glob of something came falling out of the showerhead. I closed my eyes so that I couldn't see it as it snaked its way down the drain! This is an adventure, I told myself, and cold water is good for the skin! After my very cold shower and an application of a thick layer of mosquito repellant, I walked up the hill to the main house, where food was being prepared for me. I realized that I was the only one in my little abode, and that other "guests," such as they were, stayed in rooms in the main house. I later found out that those were extremely tiny rooms, and the ASA organizer had felt that this little house would give me more space during my long stay.

The television was on, and they were broadcasting the ceremonies for inauguration of the new president of Ghana. The celebration included addresses from the heads of several African nations, as well as entertainment by various drummers. While viewing all of this fanfare, an unbelievable sadness came over me, and I tried to stifle quiet tears. I was successful, in that there was only an initial slight moistness apparent around my eyes. After the ladies finished preparing my very spicy fish and rice, I was invited to the table. I ate in silence as this huge knot began to fill in my throat, heralding the arrival of tears. I was able to hold them back for most of my meal.

The tears must have filled me up because I was unable to eat all of the spicy, but delicious, fish. Unfortunately, bits of water began to leak through my eyelids as I moved from the table to the couch. I was reminded of my trip to Germany at the tender age of twenty-one, and the absolute aloneness that I felt on my first day in Bonn.

Vera, the weekend manager of the guest house, came over to me and asked sweetly, "Are you okay?"

That was all that it took for the deluge to start streaming down my face. She retrieved some tissues for me and suggested that we go for a walk to see the hospital where I would be working. During the walk, I began to feel so much better as we each spoke of our families and the circuitous paths that we had traveled in our lives. Vera had been born in a small rural village in Uganda. Her family had suffered at the hands of the country's dictator. Hearing that her village was soon to be ravaged by marauding militia, her father gathered everyone up to try to escape.

She was the only one in her family to successfully make it to Ghana, with the aid of some missionaries. It was in their school that she was educated and taught the basics of household management. This was how she was able to obtain a job in the Dean's guest house, where I was staying, as its weekend staff manager. After approximately thirty minutes, Dr. H. Addoo, the African liaison for the ASA, and his daughter, Ruth (yes, our names are the same), came driving down the road. He offered and I accepted a trip to the town of Tema to see his older daughter, who was in boarding school and needed some shoes that had been left at home. They were quite generous with their time and pointed out all of the sights along the way.

When we arrived on the campus, I was struck by the "universality" of teenagers. Their looks, mannerisms, and obvious flirtations with the opposite sex were no different than I had seen when my girls and their friends were this age. This naturally brought a smile to my face! After we left Tema, Dr. Addoo drove me through the University of Ghana at Legon. The layout was of a typical college campus but only a few of the buildings had that "college look." No students could be seen milling around, probably due to the holiday festivities surrounding the inauguration. Upon returning to Accra, I watched "Mission Impossible II" on my DVD, and that was exciting and a good end to my day.

The next morning, the full-time manager arrived and pointed out the valves located in the back of my closet which controlled water temperature. After he left, I was excited to be able to take a hot shower. After turning on the hot water, I looked up briefly and saw another brown glob coming down from the shower head; I quickly closed my eyes and let it wash down the drain. Again, I reminded myself that this was an adventure and, brown globs or not, I was taking a hot shower at last. The day was filled with section meetings in the anesthesiology department, the Ghanaian medical-dental council, and the U.S. Embassy. Driving through nightmarish traffic could have severely dampened my mood had I not been so engaged with the many sights along the way. People young and old were busy selling their wares -- plastic bags of water, clothes, snacks, and boom boxes. It felt as though I was in a drive-through mega mart! All of these products were carried on the heads of the women, in plastic buckets, flat containers, or tied together with strings. Surprisingly, I saw no baskets, which is what my mind's eye said was the carrier of the day in Africa. I was famished when I arrived back at the Dean's guest house and was delighted to see lunch of chicken and french fries, steaming hot.

I decided to review my lecture series early because I wanted to be totally free when Jarrett called later. After I finished, I decided to lie down on my bed under the mosquito netting for a short rest. After a few minutes, I began to feel pretty blue, and my departure date of January 28 seemed a long time away. I took out my family pictures and my love plaque from Jarrett, but at that moment, those items were increasing my loneliness! I would have paid every penny that I owned just to feel Jarrett's feet or listen to Eriela's humor, or to talk with Jai about whomever her current love interest happened to be. I always tried to put on a cheery, strong face when I was around people, but it was all an act. My family and friends are so dear to me, and I ached for them all. I wished that I weren't so stubborn because it was keeping me from getting up and leaving right at that moment! My innate sense of responsibility mandated that I see a task through to completion and that meant January 28.

Dinnertime arrived, and as I waited for the cook to finish, I noticed the largest mosquito known to man trying to burrow through my extremely thick support hose, which covered an equally thick layer of mosquito repellant! Were these insects using the repellant as growth hormone? I was certain that a bruise would appear on my thigh after the force I used to kill that big rascal! I rushed through my meal in anticipation of my phone call from home -- which never came! After waiting for an hour, I returned to my little hovel down the hill, threw myself across the bed, and cried uncontrollably.

Allowing myself a few minutes of this pity party, I said to myself, "Ruth, something must be wrong! Jarrett would never miss calling you at the appointed time!"

I washed my face and went back up to the house. Upon entering, I asked one of the young workers to give me the phone number, with the intention of comparing it to the list I had been given prior to my arrival by the ASA. She haltingly began by saying, "I tink it is ..."

I screamed, "Don't think, tell me exactly!"

The poor girl was shaking in her boots before this crazed woman standing in front of her questioning her about numbers. Vera came in and gave me the correct number, which did not appear on any of the lists I had received. I decided to call my husband's office, collect. To my chagrin, there was a temp working that day. Upon hearing the operator announce that Dr. Swat was calling, she immediately said,

"He is not here," and hung up.

I was furious! I then made a collect call to my own secretary, who thankfully accepted the charges. I began crying all over again while telling her that I had not been able to reach Jarrett. Also, I began pleading for her not to tell anyone of my emotional state. She told me not to worry and that she would find my husband and give him the correct number. He called within five minutes, and all was again right in my world! The primary business for me the next day would be to obtain a calling card that I could use anywhere in Ghana!

Upon my arrival at the hospital, I realized that politics were as rampant there as they had been back in the States. The chairwoman, who was in her last month of a three-month chair cycle, decided that it was a waste of time having me there to teach cardiac anesthesia when there were so many infectious disease problems in Africa! She grudgingly agreed to allow the residents to come to my lecture series. It was not quite so easy to get her approval to allow them into the cardiac operating room. After a lengthy discussion with Dr. Addoo, the ASA liaison, and the other anesthesiologists, she agreed to allow the residents to come to the operating suite one at a time while I was there. I'm happy that I had been in touch with my "rock," Jarrett, the day before, so that her disdain did not bother me.

The day in the operating room had an auspicious start and a rapid stop because they realized that they only had two units of blood available for a major thoracoabdominal aneurysm repair, which in our operating room, required the use of many, many units of blood and blood products. The case had to be postponed for several days to allow them to find an additional four units of blood. The residents were extremely happy to be a part of my lecture series and to have a look inside the cardiac operating suite.

As the days went on, I noted the paucity of supplies available to them for all of their surgeries. Patient operating-table linens were quite threadbare and had several holes with rudimentary patches, which were also beginning to show gaping holes. Patients had to pay for and bring to the hospital all the necessary surgical supplies, such as intravenous fluids, catheters, tubing, and urinary catheter equipment, prior to being brought into the room. People lay in open hallways, some open to the outside, while waiting to be seen. On my tour, I saw a woman whose thyroid goiter was larger than her neck, with no apparent separation from her chest. When I asked to take a picture, she initially refused through my interpreter because she had paid all the money she could afford for the procedure. She was assured that there was no cost associated and allowed me to photograph her.

The cardiac unit was better equipped, primarily because the chief surgeon had personally helped build the facility's bricks and mortar and received the majority of the equipment from a hospital in Germany where he had trained. The intensive care unit was small, with beds situated along the walls as well as in the center of the room. The surgeon and anesthesiologists were quite skilled in managing the repair of major pediatric anomalies that I had only read about. Among these were bronchopleural fistula, tetralogy of Fallot, foreign body removals from the lungs, and other cardiothoracic procedures, with phenomenal results using what we would have called outdated equipment!

The day did arrive wherein they had been able to reserve six units of blood for the thoracic aneurysm case that had been delayed early on. They had decided that I should do the anesthetic management! I had brought some equipment with me to use and had left the room setup to the in-house anesthesiology team. I had attended a surgical conference that was going on in another part of the hospital and had run over to the cardiac center at its conclusion.

Time was of the essence, and I had to utilize their setup, with the addition of a few more monitoring devices and catheters that were left for me to insert. Unfortunately, their flexible bronchoscope was too large to fit down inside the endobronchial tube, so I used clinical signs to verify the tube's position. They were surprised with the ease and speed of my insertion of the remaining central catheters and monitors. I heard whispered gasps and comments as I quickly and expertly finished up. After prepping and draping, the case was able to begin, despite the unavailability of key personnel who had other hospital responsibilities. For example, the Cell Saver technician would not be available. He was tasked with running the dialysis machine somewhere else in the hospital. With the paucity of available blood, his talents would be sorely missed during this procedure.

The case appeared to be going well, with minimal instability of vital signs and data from advanced cardiac and pulmonary monitors. I began to notice some drift in the cardiac monitors without any great blood loss. I began checking indices of cardiac function, which were also beginning to decline. I then realized that the blood canisters that contained blood from the operative field were hidden behind some poles and were practically full! In addition to these problems, the left lung had begun to slowly inflate and interfere with the surgeon's ability to see the operative field. Fortunately, I had two anesthesiologists and one nurse anesthetist in the room. I tasked each of them to handle specific problem areas, such as the expanding lung, the fluid replacement, and the drawing up of medicines for me to administer.

The surgeon completed his repair of the aorta way before we were able to catch up on fluid replacement volume. The small-gauge intravenous catheters that had been placed prior to my arrival were woefully inadequate for rapid replacement of large volumes of fluids.

He kept saying that he really needed to remove the clamp, otherwise the patient would end up paralyzed. I knew from experience that this was a huge complication of prolonged ischemia (lack of blood flow). I finally placed the patient in the head down position required for aortic clamp removal. As expected, the patient's vital signs took a nosedive, especially the blood pressure! It took every bit of clinical acumen and pharmacological magic to bring that patient safely through the unclamping of the aorta with a return to normal vital signs. He awoke the next day able to breathe, move, and urinate on his own!

The surgeon was so impressed with his patient's outcome that he asked me to give a conference to the surgical department on the management of thoracoabdominal aneurysm repairs. I found that they did only two or three per year, mostly with disastrous results. We, on the other hand, would do two or three per day in my operating room at home!

30 - DELIRIUM

My loneliness quotient decreased significantly because of interesting outings in the city and countryside. My residents took me on a tour of the surrounding area to see the natural gardens and the wares of local carvers and metal workers. Their homes were part lean-to sheds and part display cases for their handmade creations. There was no set price for anything, and bargaining appeared to be the only way to do business. I felt guilty if one of my students refused to have me pay an amount that they felt was too high. They would begin negotiations in their dialect until they settled on an appropriate amount. On occasion, I would feign ignorance so as to give a larger bill denomination without accepting change, to assuage my guilt! Whenever little children were around, I would freely pass out coloring books, crayons, pencils, and pencil sharpeners. The pencil sharpeners were really a hit! I guessed that they had only seen their occasional pencils sharpened with a knife. Seeing the joy on their faces made the previous hassle of heavy bags and porters trying to get money out of me worth the effort!

Also during my stay, the National Dental Examination was being held, and the Dean's guest house served as the luncheon location for participants. It was at this time that I was witness to the haughtiness displayed between the "classes" of people. One of the women dentists in particular was extremely rude and nasty to the people who were serving us. She went as far as throwing the food on the floor and demanding that they clean it up because it was unfit for her to eat. She screamed at the poor waiter and called him all kinds of ugly names because she didn't like the food. No one in the room seemed bothered by this display! When I brought it up with the house manager, he stated that "the professors can talk to us any way they want, and we have to always bow to them and their wishes." In his mind, it was expected. Here I was in the twenty-first century being transported back to Jim Crow days of Black servitude! The only difference was that now it was Black on Black denigration! What he did not expect was that I, too, was a professor! When he found out, he was very proud that he had an American Professor as his friend.

It was such a treat to be in the company of all of these professionals from across Ghana and hear their stories. Unfortunately, I let my guard down and was not as vigilant as I should have been about my water intake. I noted after my lunch meal that my appetite had gone the way of the dodo bird by dinner time! Queasiness and a deluge of diarrhea set in by 9:00 p.m. I tried to stop it by taking Pepto Bismol, but that was not to be. After episodic trips to the toilet every thirty to forty-five minutes, I was certain that I had been poisoned! Having been told previously that they wore brown to funerals, I noted the brown towels hanging in my bathroom and the brown stripes on the linen, and I was certain that they were preparing for my funeral. By 2:00 a.m., a full-blown psychosis had set in, and my ability to think clearly was completely gone! I must have been inside a Tarzan movie because I heard all the drums and whoops around the fire that the natives used when preparing to burn someone at the stake. By 4:00 a.m., I was as weak as a newborn colt who was trying to learn to stand on weak legs. I began to prepare my bags, as I quietly cleaned my body so as to catch them by surprise while I escaped! I knew Dr. Addoo was on call at the hospital, but it was a dark, lonely, and treacherous hike -- even if I could get away from those who were guarding the house. I packed my money, IV fluids, my daughter's favorite blue pants, DVD player, and passport in preparation to flee the country. Everything else would have to remain in Africa. I required rest between each item that I placed in the suitcase. My brain had officially turned to mush. By 5:45 a.m., the night sounds began to recede from my head as dawn's light began to peek through my curtains. I began to hear the usual bird sounds of the morning but was certain that they were imitations by the people outside waiting to ambush me! I heard a car traveling down the road but was too afraid to pull back my curtain to look. Finally I heard a car horn beep directly outside and peeked to see, to my relief, that Dr. Addoo was sitting behind the wheel.

I grabbed my bag and must have been quite a sight to poor Dr. Addoo as I ran to his car and screamed, "You have to take me to the airport."

"What's wrong?" he asked.

"I'm sick, and I have to go home!" I babbled on, almost incoherently.

He said, "Let me take you inside so that I can examine you"

I replied "No, they are trying to kill me!"

He could see that I was certainly not thinking clearly, as I even turned down his request to take me to the hospital. Obviously all medical acumen had left my brain. In my dehydrated state, a transatlantic flight would have killed me! After calling his daughter to tell her that we were cancelling our trip to the coast, he finally convinced me to go to his home. When we arrived, he checked my vital signs and found that my pulse was racing at a rate of 120 and my blood pressure was up to 145/85. He offered, and I sipped, some rehydration fluid after he found out that I had not been vomiting. Within minutes, I was erupting like Mt. St. Helens with pink frothy fluid. This really frightened him since he had not gotten the Pepto Bismol history. He was now thinking that I had a bad case of malaria, resulting in blood tinged vomit! I retched and brought up everything except my toes, after which my stomach felt better than it had felt in fourteen hours! I continued to refuse a trip to the hospital. He tried to reason with me that I needed to replace all of the fluids that I had lost.

I replied, "I have fluid and IV supplies in my suitcase!"

He said, "I have no local anesthetic or anything to put an IV into you with."

I said, "I don't need any local. You are an anesthesiologist; just put in the catheter that I have in my bag!"

While he was retrieving the supplies, I struggled to his phone and awakened my poor husband at 2:00 a.m. Houston time with the following words.

"Jarrett, I'm dying. Call American Express and have them medevac me out of here. Call the American Embassy and ask for help." I later found out that Jarret did indeed call all of these places, in addition to a friend in Greece, to seek help for me! American

Express informed him that they could fly me to the safest and closest hospital in Europe, but not to the United States after speaking with an attending physician in Africa! Our friend in Greece found that there was only one flight every other day to Ghana. They then tried to construct another rescue plan, involving Jarrett's travel to Amsterdam with my subsequent transfer from Africa. That could not be effected either!

My fluid and electrolyte balance were so out of whack that I couldn't put together a reasonably coherent thought! Dr. Addoo came back and started my IV fluid, and he also called one of his colleagues over. By the time he arrived, I had received a liter of fluid and was coming back to my right mind. I requested some applesauce, and he went out and came back with some thick apple juice, which I sipped slowly. It stayed down, and the crisis seemed to be subsiding.

We decided to go out somewhere in search of a hot lunch. Unfortunately, the first few restaurants that he tried were closed. We finally happened upon a small café that purported to have some grilled chicken, which arrived at our table dripping with grease. I took off the skin and managed to get down a few bites, followed by sips from the can of Coke that I swirled to flatten out some of the gas. We then went in search of a cell phone to buy, but were informed that there was no guarantee that a phone would work in the region where we were located. So alas, we did not get a cell phone. I asked Dr. Addoo to take me to a hotel, but he wouldn't do that because it was so far away from him. He was concerned that he would not be able to reach me if I became ill during the night. I was so disappointed because I wanted to be able to call Jarrett from the hotel and not have to go into town in search of a phone to use my calling card. We stopped back by Dr. Addoo's home, so I could call Jarrett and let him know that I was better. I reluctantly agreed to go back to the Dean's guest house.

Evening arrived, and Julie came down to tell me that dinner was ready. I told her that I could not eat. She left and came back with Samantha, insisting that I needed to eat something.

I said, "Can you make me some soup with small amounts of chicken and rice in it, please?"

They looked at me quizzically and left. When they returned, they had an oversized plate of curry chicken, whose spices were assaulting my nostrils and burning my eyes, along with a huge plate of white rice! I took a teaspoon of chicken with its curry sauce, placed it over a small portion of rice, and ate half of it.

The ladies looked at each other and said, "Seuupe!"

They thought that my little bite was what I meant by soup! I survived the night and, though still weak, was well enough to go to church the next morning. The house manager and his nephews came by to pick me up in his car, and off we went.

The ladies were all decked out in their finest multicolored wrap dresses, with matching fabric head wraps sporting feathers, ribbons, and jewels. The church building was partially Western in nature, in that it had a megawatt sound system, but the outer walls were nonexistent! The service itself was similar to Baptist services that I had attended back home in the States. It was good to be in the house of the Lord after the ordeal that I had just experienced.

My trip to Cape Coast was rescheduled for later that week, but Dr. Addoo's daughter could not accompany us since she was in school. The chief surgeon gave us the use of his car, as well as spending money for the trip! As we traveled along the coast, the gray mist coming off the water and the cloudy sky made me think that this must have been what greeted the Africans who were sold into slavery and bound for the ships carrying them across the Atlantic. The sun had come out in full force when we made it to our first stop, a gorgeous resort, which belonged to a Black African! It was fabulous! We had a delightful lunch prior to proceeding on our trip to Cape Coast and the slave castles.

Upon reaching the castles, we needed to purchase entrance tickets. There was a marked difference in price for tourists and natives. Dr. Addoo, who was the product of a mixed marriage, had very fair skin and was deemed to be a tourist! He had to speak to them in three different dialects before they would believe him and give him his correct fee!

I learned that the gigantic, white stoned building with its numerous windows had been home to the captains of the slave ships when the slave trade was at its height. We were led down into a lower basement area, where the male slaves were kept. It was approximately thirty feet long and five feet wide, with one portal for light minimally visible at its highest point. There was a snake-like center groove in the floor that meandered down to another small outlet, which was used for the men's bodily waste products. Slave men were crowded in by the hundreds, and there was only space for standing; there would be no lying down prior to being led out to the slave ships, whose passageway was underneath the holding floor for the women.

The slave women had somewhat similar accommodations, with a smidgen more light and grated areas in the floor where they could look through and see the men walking past them out toward the ships. There were also stairs which led up to the slave captains' quarters, which they utilized to go down and select a woman when their sexual urges needed satisfaction.

We were also shown the tiny two-sectioned prison. The front section, which had light from the outside and a pass-through for food, was used for white pirates or other non-African criminals. The back section, which was used for the unruly African slaves, had no light and no pass-through for food. The only way out for them was death, wherein their dead bodies would be periodically removed to make way for new, doomed detainees. I could almost still smell the stench of rotting flesh from those years back. Even though it was noontime, I could barely see my hands in front of my face while back there. What a stark contrast to the hundreds of windows which lit up the castle.

There was also a torture room, which showed the variety of shackles, clamps, spiked metal balls, and stalls used for beatings. The current-day Africans had painted a sign on the door that led out to the white sandy beach and crystalline blue waters; their forebearers had marched through this door on their way to the slave ships. The sign read, "Door of No Return."

We were scheduled to stop at another slave castle on the way back, but this detailed look at man's inhumanity to man had been enough for me.

On the road back to Accra, we passed many crowded areas of closely packed housing, most of which had tin roofs and the look of destitution. One area, which had numerous goats grazing about, had an ungodly odor that permeated the air for miles. Most people in these areas seemed to have flip-flops as their only shoe gear. We passed an occasional truck filled with boxes of presumed electronics, with addressees named as far as away as Alexandria, Virginia! Thievery was alive and well! Entrepreneurs were also evident in some of the buildings that we passed.

There was a sign on the front of a five-by-ten-foot stand that stated, "Furniture for sale." A large sectional sofa sat partially inside the stand, but mostly on the outside. As we drove past, I couldn't see if there could be room for any other furniture!

After three weeks, my lecture series was completely finished, and I was ready to return home. I treated my residents to lunch at the one hotel of which I was aware. There was a delay in seating us, so I decided to browse inside the gift shop while I was waiting and saw some items that I wanted to take back home. I made a mental note to pick them up after lunch. This was the first time that I could use my American Express card, and I was going to do it justice!

While waiting to be checked out, I noticed the bright cheery smiles that were being given to the white patrons by the African personnel working at the desk. The surly undertone that greeted me when it was my turn was almost palpable!

As I handed the clerk my card, she snidely remarked, "This purchase will have to be verified with the operator."

I said, "Okay," in a calm tone while she angrily spoke with the Amex operator.

"What is up with her?" I said to myself.

She then turned to me and quoted an amount that was fifty cents more in U.S. dollars than in Ghanain cedis. I asked, in my most polite tone, why I was being charged more that the stated amount of my purchase.

She stated in her surly tone, "It is easier for them to understand round numbers!"

I then said, with all of the attitude that I could muster, "Two thousand cedis is a lot of money to the average Ghanaian. You will NOT charge that to my card!"

She glared at me and said that then she would have to redo the entire transaction. I responded with a very steely glare and equally haughty tone, "Do it!"

My residents were doing high fives in the corner at her comeuppance! This was the second time in less than three weeks that I had been exposed to discrimination by others whose roots were the same as mine, and I was having none of it!

31 - HOMEWARD BOUND

By Friday, I was determined to leave a couple of days early. All the anesthesia and surgical personnel tried to persuade me to stay longer, but I was ready to go Home! On the day of my departure, the surgeon suggested that I use the hospital ambulance to take me to the airport and check my bags because the wait would be hours there. They could bring me back to wait at the guest house until it was closer to time for me to leave. I graciously accepted. Upon my return from the airport, I took my second shower of the day. Later that evening, my trusty ambulance, with its ability to bypass crowds on one-way streets, returned me to the airport. I was waiting in the KLM business class lounge and heard my flight called.

One of the hostesses came over to me and said," KLM would send someone to escort you when the time comes because the gate is quite a ways away. You should stay comfortably seated until that time."

I tried very hard to adhere to her directions, but after the fifth call for my flight, I got up and asked for directions to the gate. It took me approximately twenty minutes to reach the gate, which seemed at this moment to have a thousand people waiting! I did note that toward the front, there were arrows to several different gates. Finally, someone came over a bullhorn and began giving instructions, none of which I understood, primarily because the sound was not loud enough. Finally I saw a wave of humanity moving forward. I started moving too! Suddenly, I heard my name! I turned and saw a group of Caucasians, who turned out to be visiting anesthesiologists who had been volunteering down in Kumasi, Ghana. They had heard about our thoracic aneurysm repair and had been trying to reach me during my multiple trips to the airport earlier in the day. We chatted briefly, with plans to visit en route to the U.S. They were going to do a little sightseeing in Amsterdam, but I was NOT going anywhere far from my ride home! Since I had paid the exorbitant fare to upgrade to business class, I didn't have a chance to speak with the other anesthesiologists again.

On the flight home, the flight attendant smiled when I questioned the safety of the water that she was handing out and assured me that it was safe. I was determined to arrive home safely, in good health, and on time!

32 - ON UNITED STATES SOIL

After walking out of the double doors from the customs area, Jarrett ducked under the ropes and picked me up, giving me the longest kiss known to man! I guess he must have missed me as much as I missed him! I told him that I did not want anyone to know that I was back home in the States. He readily agreed.

When we arrived home, he drew a nice warm bath for me to soak in prior to him bathing me. It felt so good to have such loving, tender care. When I got out of the tub, there appeared to be two inches of dirt and oil residue, even though I had taken two showers prior to leaving Africa!

Life went back to the normal crazy at work. The workday was consistently twelve to sixteen hours long! After a particularly long non-call day, wherein I had arrived at 6:00 a.m. and left at 3:00 a.m. the following morning, pure exhaustion set in, and I could not put clothes on to be ready for work at 7:00 a.m.! I called in and told them that I needed a few more hours of rest and would be in at 11:00 a.m. There was no fuss from anyone because I am sure that they had all heard of the horrendous day and night that I had just had. When 11:00 arrived and I told them that I was on my way, they told me not to come because they had it covered. I promptly went back to bed and slept until the next morning! After breakfast, I went back to sleep and awakened at 2:00 a.m. that Sunday morning, finding to my surprise that Jarrett was also awake. We began to discuss our lives and the constant drain on both our bodies. After telling him over the past several weeks of my experiences in Africa and the satisfaction that most of the professionals had with their lives, we almost questioned simultaneously, "When is enough enough?"

He said, "Baby, I think it is time for you to stop working. Jai is in her last year of college, and we have saved enough to live on with one income."

The next morning, I scheduled a meeting with my section chief to let her know of my plans. She said that she also had some good news for me and wanted to know who should go first. I told her that she should share her news first. She seemed almost giddy as she put on her biggest smile and said, "I have obtained a 30 percent increase in all faculty salaries, and it will be retroactive to January 1."

I said, "That's great! I am giving you six months' notice."

She looked at me incredulously and said, "Isn't Jai still in college?"

I responded, "Yes."

She questioned further, "What are you going to do about that?" I stated, "Pay for it."

With that, I stood up and proceeded out of the door. The meeting was over, as far as I was concerned. The room was so quiet when I left that a dewdrop from a rose petal could be heard in the distance! I was finally in charge of my own destiny! When word spread around the operating room suite that I was leaving, various surgeons would walk up to me and ask,

"What are you going to do?" My response was always the same, "Become a doctor's wife, like your wife!"

§ § §

"Power is the only thing respected in our American System." A. Philip Randolph

EPILOGUE

As a child, I was surrounded by family and friends who were just like me. This cocoon of normalcy shielded me from the tumult of civil rights changes going on around me in the United States. When I should have been old enough to really appreciate the struggle, the indifference and feelings of immortality of young adulthood kept me on the sidelines. I now can look at the tremendous gift that I was given through the sacrifice of others. The laws of the land, including civil and women's rights, are continually being challenged. Though we have no Black and White Freedom Riders, we had enough committed Black and White voters to elect our first Black President, Barack Obama. We must continue to educate our children on our mutual pasts and the tenuous thread of our hard-fought-for civil liberties. With this educational process, they will not be lulled into a false sense of security and will continue to do the work required to keep their rights. They will not joyously sing "Oh Susanna," as I was taught, because they will realize that it was meant as a racial slur, performed in Blackface, to marginalize Black slaves and celebrate vicious killings of these slaves.

As a woman and a Black person, I had to put in extraordinary effort and hard work in order to succeed. I learned later in life that I needed to develop goals and objectives, along with the discipline required to actualize them. Fortunately, I was able to have some fun along my journey and to develop some good relationships. No matter how hard things look at any given moment – in our lives or in the life of the world – our destinies are in our own hands. My faith allows me to realize that God had this plan for me. Remember that as long as we work HIS plan, our vital signs are and will remain stable!

"We Shall Overcome!"

ABOUT THE AUTHOR

Dr. M. Ruth Swafford was born at a time in Tennessee when Jim Crow laws were strictly adhered to and enforced. Her education took her from the segregated halls of Manassas High School to Howard University where she obtained her B.A. degree in German. After working in the private sector for a number of years, she decided to return to Howard University College of Medicine from which she obtained her M.D. degree. She also completed her Anesthesiology residency at Howard University hospital before moving on to do advanced training in Cardiothoracic and Vascular Anesthesiology. She became a practicing Cardiothoracic and Vascular Anesthesiologist. Upon retiring, she decided to pen this, her memoir.

Made in the USA
Lexington, KY
15 June 2016